EVER PRESENT

Real Stories of God's Presence Through Trials and Triumphs

PATRICIA CAMERON

GREEN
LEAF
INK

Holy Bible, New International Version®, NIV®. Copyright © 1973, 1978, 1984, 2011 by Biblica, Inc.® Used by permission. All rights reserved worldwide.

The Holy Bible, English Standard Version, ESV®. Text edition: 2016. Copyright © 2001 by Crossway Bibles, a publishing ministry of Good News Publishers.

Scriptures marked NLT are taken from the Holy Bible, New Living Translation. Copyright © 1996, 2004, 2015 by Tyndale House Foundation. Used by permission of Tyndale House Publishers, Inc., Carol Stream, Illinois 60188. All rights reserved.

Scriptures marked NKJV are taken from the New King James Version®. Copyright © 1982 by Thomas Nelson. Used by permission. All rights reserved.

Scriptures marked NASB are taken from the New American Standard Bible®. Copyright © 1960, 1971, 1977, 1995, 2020 by The Lockman Foundation. All rights reserved.

Scriptures marked NASB1995 are taken from the New American Standard Bible®. Copyright © 1960, 1971, 1977, 1995 by The Lockman Foundation. All rights reserved.

Scriptures marked CSB are taken from the Christian Standard Bible. Copyright © 2017 by Holman Bible Publishers. Used by permission. Christian Standard Bible® and CSB® are federally registered trademarks of Holman Bible Publishers, all rights reserved.

For more information, email patricia@greenleafink.com. Or find out more at patriciacameronwrites.com.

ISBN: 979-8-89316-385-8 - Paperback
ISBN: 979-8-89316-386-5 - Hardcover
ISBN: 979-8-89316-384-1 - eBook

DEDICATION

I dedicate this book to my three sons:

Connor, Garrett and Parker

You are the heartbeat of my life, filling my days with joy and adventure. Thank you for your support in this new one.

May you always love and abide in the Lord, learn from life's challenges and live your dream.

CONTENTS

INTRODUCTION

D o you ever wonder where God is in your story? Those days or months when you need Him the most? Have you wrestled with the idea of God being good? Do you sometimes feel alone, even in a crowded room, unsure if God is with you? You are not alone.

Studies show everyone needs to feel a connection with someone or something. We want to have a sense of value and self-worth. We have a desire for God and Heaven even though we don't always recognize it.

In essence, our deepest need is a relationship with a Holy God who offers profound meaning, worth and fulfillment.

My friend, God also knows what we need most. Because of that, we can know He is with us, too. We desperately need the presence of the living God in our lives. We need a glimpse of who He is.

Though we know God is out there, we can't always feel Him with us, which may cause us to feel alone and afraid or confused. We could even be too busy to notice. But how often do we know His nearness?

God walks alongside us in our daily routine, when we're fighting our life's battles, and in every situation in between. I've experienced it.

Sadly, many still search for Him, not always knowing what they're searching for.

We don't have to search far. He accompanies us through everyday moments. We just need to learn to recognize Him. This book will show you how to realize God's presence in your everyday lives. It's filled with real people and real stories that point you to a real God.

The book of Luke records many eyewitness accounts of people who had been with Jesus. Through the stories on the following pages, you will also witness God's work in the lives of people just like you and me. Each person tells a story of his or her interaction with Almighty God, who's also close enough to be personal. As they walk, see and listen, they experience God's redeeming work and healing in their lives.

I hope that in these stories, you will catch a glimpse of who God is and the hope He offers. May they remind you there is hope and joy in experiencing God's presence and nearness. As you read, may you grow closer to God, who lovingly pursues and guides you.

Let God transform you into a new person by changing the way you think (see Romans 12:2 NLT).

This book has long been an idea of mine. I've wanted to capture stories that have encouraged and inspired me. And God has delivered. He has encouraged me through the many stories in the Bible of His nearness, His restoration and His love. He has encouraged me through stories of real people who experienced God's presence as an integral part of their lives.

Having an awareness of God's presence in our lives will uplift, inspire and change us for the better.

Don't miss hearing from Him through the stories of everyday people in ordinary ways. Let them move you to a deeper relationship with Jesus that will provide meaning and fulfillment. Each chapter opens with relatable quotes, scriptures and songs to remind you of a real God who loves you and will never leave you.

I challenge you to look for God in your story, whatever the day brings. Wherever you may go, He remains ever present and always by your side. He knows what's happening. He moves toward you when you run. You may not see it at the time, but He works on your behalf.

I pray you will experience God's presence like a warm embrace on a cold winter night and be reminded of who He is. Remember His words. Remember what He's done throughout the day: when you stand, when you sit, when you walk and when you lie down.

In God's nearness, find joy. Find hope. Find peace.

CHAPTER ONE

God Is in Your Story

Quote:

"We can't think rightly of God until we begin to think of Him as always being there — and being there first!"

— A. W. Tozer, Mornings with Tozer, April 25

Scripture:

"As I was with Moses, so I will be with you; I will never leave you nor forsake you" (Joshua 1:5 NIV).

Songs:

"How He Loves" by David Crowder Band

"God Is In This Story" by Katy Nichole & Big Daddy Weave

While reading the story of Gideon in Judges 6 and 7, I saw myself in scripture one day.

I didn't see myself in the way you might think—as the prophet Gideon leading his people to conquer the cruel Midianites.

I didn't see myself in how Gideon asked God for a sign (remember the fleece story in Judges 6:36–40?). I've certainly done my share of that, though.

I saw myself in a man given to fear—a man who acted faithlessly. I saw myself in a man full of questions, a man who doubted God.

But then I saw God in this story. God knew Gideon. He knew his shortcomings, and He knew his fears and doubts. God didn't reprimand or lecture Gideon. Instead, He acted patiently. He walked beside Gideon and encouraged him.

God knew Gideon needed a glimpse of who He was.

And Gideon saw God defeat 120,000 Midianites with 300 Israelite soldiers whose weapons were only trumpets and jars with torches inside.

Glimpses of God

I have seen glimpses of God at work throughout my life. I didn't always know it at the time, but when I reflect on it, God stood close. He has been forever faithful. He has been my rock, my confidant, my provider. God's army wasn't in full view, but I know it was there. He has seen me through:

MY CONFUSING and insecure years as a young girl. Growing up in a loving, Christian home introduced me to Jesus and grounded me in my faith. Because of my upbringing, I knew I needed Jesus.

TRAGEDY IN my family. My dad suffered a debilitating accident when he was 36 and I was five. We desperately needed God. Dad didn't know Jesus, and at one point, he was near death. But God saved Daddy in more ways than one. He accepted Christ as his Lord and Savior two years later. After a six-month hospital stay and rehab in Boston, Dad came home with prosthetic legs. Both he and my mom worked hard, put their trust in the Lord and led our family by example.

HEARTBREAK FROM an unwanted divorce. As a young wife learning my husband had been unfaithful, I cried out to God, asking why. Divorced and devastated, I drew close to the only one I knew who could comfort me: Jesus. God taught me so much in those next few years. As I struggled with being alone, He was by my side. Jesus became so real to me. He taught me to forgive and gave me the healing I desperately needed. With that came the ability to move on.

THE DEVASTATING LOSS of a nephew who died at the hands of an abusive stepfather.

A SEASON OF PRAYING when a friend asked me to intercede for someone who did not know Christ. I prayed, not knowing her friend would one day be my best friend and husband. God drew him in, and he gave his life to Christ.

THE LOSS of a beloved best friend due to cancer.

REPEATED MISCARRIAGES and grief when our infant daughter died at birth due to Potter syndrome, a rare disorder with zero chance of survival. God carried us through that season with a community of friends who surrounded us with love and encouragement. And He gave us the strength to pick ourselves up and embrace life again.

THE ADOPTION process. We experienced God's wonderful blessing of two sons. Plus, God's protection and gift through my pregnancy and birth of our third son.

THE AGONIZING WEEK and final day when my family's world changed forever. Everything shifted the day we said goodbye to my soul's companion, my husband. In my deepest pain, I had to decide whether I trusted God or not. To decide if what I knew in my head was what I believed in my heart. I had to trust God was who He said He was and what He said was true.

A SEASON OF QUESTIONING my life's journey. God placed a stirring in my heart to encourage and support others facing pain and loss. God inspired me to write a book about living with joy while experiencing grief. God also gave me a sense of purpose to speak about the goodness and nearness of God.

My story is one of heartbreak, fear, loss and overcoming obstacles. My story is a story of trust and forgiveness, hope and joy and laughter. It is filled with glimpses of God at work and His redeeming and refining grace.

He has been the light in my darkest moments. My hope when I was hopeless. My joy in sorrow and a spring in my dry season. Although He is the sovereign God of the universe, He's also close enough to meet my deepest needs.

I never dreamed where my journey would take me. Yes, I had dreams throughout my life. Of being a wife and mother.

Of succeeding in my career. Of growing old together with my husband. Even being a backup singer for Ronnie Milsap!

I don't regret one bit of it, for God always saw me through the good and the bad. I am thankful for every chuckle, every tear, every memory, every trip and every friendship's impact on my life.

I am thankful God showed me I could still have joy. He put people in my life, scriptures in my path and songs in my heart that encouraged and lifted me from a deep darkness that was my life for a time.

When my husband died, I thought there was no way I could do this on my own with three young boys at home. Yet, I've seen our sons grow and mature, learn to drive, begin dating and working while attending school. I couldn't be prouder of the young men they have become. With all my mistakes through the years, I wonder how we ever got to this place. My husband wasn't by my side during these impactful and pivotal years. But Jesus was.

Although I have cried out to God at various points along the way, God has always met me there. He has showered mercy and grace on me.

He has proven He is good. He is sovereign. And He is near.

God is forever faithful. I can trust that He will remain faithful. He is the Alpha and Omega, the beginning and the end. He was at the beginning of my story, and he will be with me until my final days.

I may not be grateful for every struggle or hardship or loss. But I can be grateful for this — God reigns.

I can be grateful that He has been there to sustain me. I can be grateful for every lesson I've learned along the way and am still learning.

I can be grateful for God's timing. Thank God, He is in my story. And He is in your story, too.

And He offers all of us a full and joy-filled life.

"These things I have spoken to you so that My joy may be in you, and that your joy may be made full" (John 15:11 NASB).

God gave Gideon a glimpse of who He was.

Many times, a battle has raged around me. Through these experiences, He has given me a glimpse of who He is, showing me that He positioned an army around me to surround and conquer my enemies.

He loves. He cares. He leads us and guides us. We can trust Him. He knows the bigger picture.

The Big Picture

We began the drive to my son's soccer game under a brilliant blue sky, crisp against white wispy clouds.

We stopped for a fast-food breakfast after driving one hour. While we waited in line, I entered my destination into the car's GPS. The guidance surprised me by giving me an alternative to my usual route to a city five hours away. I reasoned there must be some traffic issue that caused the reroute.

The new route directed me north where I thought we should have turned south.

I didn't trust it, so I pulled into a parking lot to get my bearings. My son beside me — oblivious to my internal dilemma — continued staring at his phone.

After I took a moment to expand the map, I saw the bigger picture.

This route took us through twists and turns and trees arching over the road in the winter landscape. Only a small part of the route was in view at first. But it got us to the same destination.

One Step at a Time

The moment I saw the bigger map, God reminded me that He had a bigger picture for me, too.

Isn't that the way with God sometimes? He uses simple tasks or circumstances to speak to us.

We may experience things that don't seem right or require us to walk a path we don't understand. Or we could even be oblivious to God's direction for us.

Even so, God's guidance is there. God sees the big picture. His plan is bigger and better than we can imagine.

We will reach our destination, although the road we travel may not be what we expect and there may be twists and turns along the way. Our doubts may delay our progress.

The truth is we don't need to know the big picture right now. I doubt we could handle it if we did.

One Plan at a Time

God is with us whenever our lives fall apart, whenever our plans don't turn out like we think they should.

When God sent Jacob down to Egypt with all his family and livestock and possessions, He didn't send him alone. He spoke to Jacob in a dream.

"Do not be afraid to go down to Egypt, for I will make you into a great nation there. I will go down to Egypt with you, and I will surely bring you back again" (Genesis 46:3b–4a NIV).

Before this vision, Jacob must have been apprehensive about moving to the land of his enemies. I feel certain he never planned to move to enemy territory.

But God doesn't just send us into the unknown. He goes with us whenever, wherever.

In those days, God's special presence was a unique thing. A few thousand years later, we have access to God the Spirit, who dwells in all believers. We get to carry Him with us wherever we go.

God has filled us with His Spirit, sealing us and promising to stay with us forever.

His presence remains with us. He is our light in the darkness, our hope when we're hopeless. He brings joy in our sorrow and meets us in our wilderness. He is King of Kings and Lord of Lords and able to meet our deepest needs. We need only look for His presence in our lives and see God in our story.

Trust God

We can trust God's guidance. We can trust He knows best. Even when we can't see it, God is working.

Let's remain focused on the journey of faith before us and stay on the path He has designed. Let us stay faithful as God in His wisdom works out the big picture for our lives.

We need not see far ahead. Jesus calls us to take one step at a time with Him.

"For now we see in a mirror dimly, but then face to face; now I know in part, but then I will know fully just as I also have been fully known" (1 Corinthians 13:12 NASB1995).

Just because His presence is not visible doesn't mean God's call and guidance for His people aren't there. His name was never mentioned in the book of Esther, a powerful story about a humble woman who saved her people from genocide. But His hand shows up all over her story. His providence is seen in the series of events that led to the salvation of the Jews.

Esther became queen. God placed her in a position to save her people. Her cousin Mordecai was confident God would deliver the Jews even if Esther didn't act. God intervened, guiding Mordecai to overhear an assassination plot against the king. Later, the king's sleepless night led to Mordecai's public recognition. Then there was a dramatic turnaround when Haman, who devised a plot to exterminate the Jewish people, hanged on his own gallows. God worked through all of these events and through the stories of these people to fulfill His promise to preserve His people (See Esther 1–10).

That goes for us, too. He works — always — in our story.

Humankind tends to place God far away, somewhere beyond our ability to comprehend, contained by space and time. But God cannot be contained.

He is not far away. He is intimately involved in His creation. We can know Him. He pursues us through His word, through our prayers and through the presence of the Holy Spirit.

Seek God's presence and you will find.

Remember the Nearness of God

Sometimes life gets so busy that we fail to see God or experience His presence. Stress and anxiety steal our days and nights. There's a place for them. At the feet of Jesus. Release them to Him.

Bring your cares, your concerns, your hurts, your dreams — all the things that trigger anxiety — and lay them at the feet of Jesus.

Jesus left this earthly life to send the Holy Spirit, who not only walks beside us but lives in us so we are never alone. He is always by our side.

CHAPTER TWO

Stress and Anxiety

Quotes:

*"Our anxiety does not empty tomorrow of its sorrows,
but only empties today of its strengths."*
— *C. H. Spurgeon*

"Worrying is like paying a debt you don't owe."
— *Mark Twain*

Scriptures:

*"And he said, 'My presence will go with you, and I
will give you rest'" (Exodus 33:14 NIV).*

*"When anxiety was great within me, your consolation
brought me joy" (Psalm 94:19 NIV).*

*"Be anxious for nothing, but in everything by prayer and
supplication with thanksgiving let your requests be made
known to God" (Philippians 4:6 NASB1995).*

Songs:

"Breathe" by Jonny Diaz
"All Joy No Stress" by Rhett Walker

I have successfully loaded a ski lift for 30-plus years. It wasn't hard. Until it was. One day, the lift got the best of me. It's a special lift — I call it the magic carpet lift. You simply enter, stand still, and wait for the carpet to take you to the place where the seat picks you up. This time, when my ski tips hit the slushy ice, my feet turned unnaturally, forcing my knees together. I fell backward and the seat hit my head. I lay there, calling, "My knees, my knees!" Now, experiencing this once was embarrassing enough. But I did the very same thing again. Twice! My son was so embarrassed.

Sometimes life just gets the best of us. We may be enjoying a normal day when we're struck by a sad moment. That moment can throw our whole day — or even week — out of whack. Maybe it's receiving a dreaded call about a family member or feeling as if things are falling apart around us.

In one month alone, my middle son ran into a barbed wire fence while riding his bike, our roof leaked, termites swarmed our neighborhood, our water heater needed to be replaced, and we found a rodent living in our attic, just to name a few! Lord help us all when those types of weeks or months rain down!

Sometimes we just need to talk to someone who understands when our hearts are heavy, our minds a cluttered mess.

I don't know all the whys and answers to our questions, but I do know that God does. He sees us, He knows us and He's beside us during our painful moments. Scripture even tells us directly that God hears our prayers.

"For the eyes of the Lord are on the righteous and his ears are attentive to their prayer" (1 Peter 3:12 NIV).

We may not always feel that He hears us, but this is truth. He *is* attentive to our prayers.

I may not have voiced the words to the Lord, "Please save my knees," but God heard the cry of my heart. My knees eventually would recover, and the young man who picked me up demonstrated patience and kindness. For that, I am grateful.

White Thread and Shoe Polish to the Rescue

I love weddings. They bring fond memories and happy times. But weddings — and human nature — are prone to glitches. Usually, they're insignificant in the grand scheme of things.

However, some weddings have a story to tell. Like Lisa's.

Two hours before the ceremony, my wedding dress caught on fire. Yes, you read that correctly. Minutes before marrying the love of my life, the dress caught on fire.

Typical of the late '80s, candles filled the stage and big hoop dresses were the thing. A lot of candles and a whole lot of dress marked that day.

While taking bridal pictures before the ceremony, the photographer asked me to move closer to the candlelight. Which I did. He then asked me to step forward. And in that moment, the lace in the big hoop of my skirt caught the wick of a votive candle on the altar. Flames shot up. It was such a large hoop that I did not immediately notice it.

Fortunately, someone else did, and she began yelling my name and waving her arms.

The photographer beat the flames out with his hand while we shared a moment of pure shock. Then he asked, "Who's the best seamstress we can get?" That seamstress was my mom.

> *My next thought (in vanity) was, I've had my hair and makeup done . . . I will not cry or fall apart.*
>
> *Mom and the pastor's wife came to the rescue with thread and white shoe polish. And no one who wasn't witness to it saw the hole from that near disaster.*

Was God with Lisa that day? You'd better believe it. If not for the hoop in her skirt, the flames would have touched her skin, making the situation much, much worse.

God protected her, and amazingly, she held it together through the ceremony.

We have God (and a hoop) to thank and a story to tell.

Worry About Many Things

In the story of Mary and Martha in Luke 10:38–42, Martha was worried about many things. I can envision it. How many people are coming? Do I have enough food? Wine? I'm running out of time. I forgot to take the roast out of the oven! Let me pick some flowers for a centerpiece. Where's my sister?! Her feelings had grown resentful, possibly aggressive. "Tell Mary to help me."

She didn't realize it at the time, but the answer to those "many things" stood a few feet from her. Jesus.

Jesus wanted her to rest at His feet. He wanted her to stop worrying and getting distracted from the most important things. But Martha fluttered around. Mary stayed at His feet. He would not take that away from Mary.

The world offers many distractions to keep us too busy to seek Jesus.

Turn Down the Volume of the World

When we chase worldly distractions, with constant noise bombarding us, we miss the gentle whispers of God's voice. We miss the joy and peace of living in His presence.

Jesus walks quietly beside us. His voice is so quiet that it is sometimes lost in the busyness around us, creating a barrier between us and our ability to hear His voice.

Until we become quiet ourselves, we do not hear it. But He is there, by our side, waiting.

The Bible paints a beautiful picture of the invitation to draw near to God. Throughout scripture, God points us to our rescue that comes through the sacrifice of Christ. Everyone is invited. The choice is up to us. We can't control a lot of things in this life, but we can control our future by this one decision.

By seeking His voice amid the chaos, we can cultivate a deeper connection with Him and truly experience the joy of living in God's presence.

Just as we do not doubt the love of our closest family and friends, even on the days we don't see or speak to each other, we don't need to doubt God's love when He seems far away. There may be quiet days with God. There may be days of laughter and days of sadness. Still, He remains near, loving and guiding us in every moment.

We need to look for God in our story. We need to remember what He has done for us and see how He has shown up and walked beside us.

I wonder how many times I've missed something because I was distracted with my "many things." Jesus is where we find joy, but we can allow our stress to steal our joy.

<u>All Joy, No Stress</u>

I heard the song "All Joy No Stress" on my drive home from my parents' house. I didn't even know the artist's name at the time, but those words clung to me like a dryer sheet on a fleece blanket. I couldn't get the prior day's mistake off my mind. I went to bed worried and woke up the same way.

Here's what happened: My friends and I had recorded a Facebook live video to tell people about my book's progress. Not wanting to stuff myself in jeans, I'd put on my most comfortable skirt. We positioned the camera so people could only see me from the waist up. Or so we thought.

I didn't even think about my skirt since it wasn't in the camera screen. To my horror and dismay, my skirt — and top of my legs — were clearly on screen. Here I was, sharing what God had done in my life while showing way too much leg! How could I have let that happen? In all my years of training people to speak on camera in my corporate job, I should have known better.

My friends tried to encourage me, saying it wasn't that bad and that no one would notice. (Thank God for friends!) But I wasn't convinced.

The true test? My mom. Of course, she noticed. I wanted to crawl into a hole. It still makes me shudder.

The song lyrics seemed to mock me that next morning. After all, my book focuses on having joy in all circumstances. I, however, was far from "all joy, no stress."

That's just like God, isn't it? I had anxiety in droves, and He sent a song to release me from that worry.

I just had to grab hold of that joy, even when I wanted to stay in my hole and pretend the embarrassing moment didn't happen.

What about you? Have you been there? Has God spoken to you through a song? Through a scripture? Or through a friend's voice of reason?

We can find joy through any circumstance. Even when our own weakness, neglect or oversight is to blame.

I've got to tell you — I had a hard time keeping my anxiety from ruining my day. But that would have been truly a waste. My stress served no purpose. I had to give it to the Lord.

All joy. No stress. We should strive to live that way and not waste the day by allowing our anxiety to get the best of us.

"A joyful heart is good medicine, but a crushed spirit dries up the bones" (Proverbs 17:22 ESV).

Just Breathe

What's on your mind? What keeps you up at night or awakens you in the early morning hours? Hopefully, it's not something causing turmoil or creating havoc. However, sometimes our own thoughts do exactly that. What is that constant worry keeping you in a state of disarray? Or the nagging voice that distracts you from your life's purpose?

Could you just take a moment to breathe and trust God? To pause and rest at Jesus' feet? Enjoy quiet time with the Lord. Leave your "worry about many things" behind. Just be with Jesus. Fill your lungs with His holy presence.

Maybe your chaos isn't as dramatic as a wedding dress catching on fire, but chaos will come. The day may turn wild. This is all the more reason to take a breath and rest in Jesus. Step away from the distractions and see goodness, experience peace and find rest in Jesus.

Jesus Is in Control

Jesus brought calm in the chaos and peace in the storm. He spoke healing to the helpless and provided plenty to the hungry. He spent time with outcasts as well as the prominent. He made Himself available to men and women alike, and He cherished children. He taught. He prayed. He wept. He loved.

And He does that for us, too. When trials, tests and temptations come, we can rest knowing He is in control. He comforts us, He fights for us, He stands with us. He remains near to us.

We can rest at night knowing that He is in control and He's available.

CHAPTER THREE

Trials, Tests and Temptations

Quotes:

*"Hardships often prepare ordinary people
for an extraordinary destiny."*

— C. S. Lewis

"I can rest at night because God is by my side and He fights for me."

— Victor Hugo

Scripture:

*"And Moses said to the people, 'Fear not, stand firm, and
see the salvation of the LORD, which he will work for you
today. For the Egyptians whom you see today, you shall
never see again. The LORD will fight for you, and you
have only to be silent'" (Exodus 14:13–14 ESV).*

Songs:

*"You've Already Won" by Shane & Shane
"Battle Belongs" by Phil Wickham*

S ometimes things don't turn out as you plan. No real secret there, right?

As my son loaded up a bed frame to take to his first "home away from home" at college, I asked him if it was secure in the back of the pickup. He casually answered yes.

However, at the first significant bump in the road, that frame sailed out of the truck and into the middle of the interstate.

He called with the news, to which I cried out to God, "Lord, not something else!"

Not knowing what else to do, he kept driving, seeing cars swerving in the lanes behind him.

The other drivers must have been stunned to see the assembled cloth-and-metal frame flying toward them. Fortunately, someone stopped and moved the obstruction to the side of the road, and no one was injured in the ordeal.

Bumps often come as an unwelcome surprise. Sometimes they come in an unexpected storm.

Riding Out the Storm

The midmorning sun shone bright, creating tiny diamonds in the water. I was on a boating excursion with two of my sons and their friends, and we were ready for a fun day of tubing and knee boarding. Because school had already begun in many areas, we were the only boat on the lake.

After a couple of hours, we noticed dark clouds brewing in the distance. The sun's brilliance stood in stark contrast to the dark shadows moving across the sky. I kept a watchful eye.

I remembered dodging storm clouds on a similar day a few years before. At that time, God's glory displayed itself, as we saw both ends of the rainbow across the lake. Trailing our water play, the rainbow remained behind us, a breathtaking scene.

This day lacked that view. To my dismay, the weather conditions changed quickly.

Bolts of lightning accompanied those dark clouds. Lots of lightning. We discussed our options and decided to try to outrun it and headed back to the marina. By the time we were halfway there, the storm was hovering directly in our path. We turned back and cruised to another part of the lake to escape the more intense part of the storm.

That option failed to deliver.

Navigating the boat to the farthest point the rental company allowed, we sat and hoped the storm would travel south of us. We were unsuccessful again, so we braced for the storm.

The rain became a wall of water that drenched us in seconds. We couldn't see anything around us except sheets of rain. Then came pounding hail. We steeled ourselves as we hunkered down under now-wet beach towels. Our sunny, hot day at the lake had become cold, scary and painful.

I tried to stay calm, but my inner resolve began to waver. Fear struck my heart. What should I do? I needed to be strong, to put forth a positive attitude. But the simple truth? I did not know what to do.

Except pray. While we tried to downplay it with our laughs and jokes, I'm pretty sure all four boys were also praying.

"I'm sure glad I know where I'm going!" one boy shouted over the noise.

A friend yelled back, "Where?"

"Heaven."

Eventually, the sky to the north lightened some, so I decided to head that way, slowly. I no longer cared whether we were breaking the boat-rental rules, we just needed to get out of the deluge.

The storm finally moved out of the area, and we breathed a sigh of relief. I replayed it in my mind, wondering what I could have done differently.

Sometimes, while in the middle of our personal storms, we also experience low visibility. We can't see what's in front of us, and we panic. Sometimes we lose our grip on reality. But no matter our storm, we can trust Jesus.

Although I didn't know the outcome, I knew that God was there with us. He knew exactly what we were going to see that day. He is attentive. He works on our behalf even when we can't see the outcome.

He took care of us and gave us as a lesson in gratitude and an experience we will never forget. After the storm? We took a break and grabbed ice cream and snacks. Then we went right back on the water and enjoyed the rest of the day on an empty lake.

Maybe God wants to show you something through your storms, too. The disciples once called out to Jesus to save them from a storm, and He delivered them (see Mark 4:35-41). Jesus protects. He delivers. Sometimes we just need to hang on and ride out the storm.

Jesus, our Lord of the seas, rides with us. We can trust Him. When we are being tested, let's trust in Jesus. Do as He says, even when it doesn't make sense.

"This is my command — be strong and courageous! Do not be afraid or discouraged. For the Lord your God is with you wherever you go" (Joshua 1:9 NLT).

An Unforgettable Journey

Three exiled Jews found themselves in the test of their lives.

King Nebuchadnezzar had a golden image built and required all people to bow down and worship it when they heard the sound of the horn, flute and other instruments. Whoever failed to worship the image would be thrown into a blazing furnace (see Daniel 3:8–25).

When these Jews — Shadrach, Meshach and Abednego — were condemned to the fire for refusing to worship the king's image, they faced their fate in peace. They didn't know how their story would end, but they knew that their God had the power to protect them. They refused to serve Nebuchadnezzar's gods even if that protection never came.

They boldly marched through the fire because they weren't alone. Their faith really did become sight, as they saw a fourth man walking with them. And they lived to tell about it. I would love to have heard their story as they returned to their homes. I imagine their awe stayed with them for the rest of their lives.

Our God is bigger than all our problems. He's right there, walking through our fire with us, too.

Losing the Way

Hundreds of years earlier, the Israelites faced a different kind of test. A test that shaped their future.

After fleeing Egypt, they made it to the edge of the land God had promised. They stood at its entrance at Kadesh Barnea — so close, yet so far away. God commanded them to follow His direction, conquer the land, and then live in the paradise He had prepared and set aside for them.

Somewhere along the journey, they lost their way.

Israelite leaders handpicked 12 men to explore the land of Canaan. Their job was simple. See what the land and the people were like and bring back some fruit. After spies returned from scouting the land, Joshua and Caleb encouraged the assembly to go possess it. They knew God had promised it and He was with them.

But the other spies told a different story.

Their fear had already defeated them. Their hearts sank with dread because of the massive walls that surrounded the cities and the giants who lived there. Their negative outlook led the rest of the community into alarm and distress. These 10 spies saw danger and turned back.

"That night all the members of the community raised their voices and wept aloud. All the Israelites grumbled against Moses and Aaron, and the whole assembly said to them, 'If only we had died in Egypt! Or in this wilderness! Why is the Lord bringing us to this land only to let us fall by the sword? Our wives and children will be taken as plunder. Wouldn't it be better for us to go back to Egypt?'" (Numbers 14:1–3 NIV).

Their mistake?

The Israelites listened to the wrong voices, ignoring God's direction. They decided it was too risky to cross the Jordan into the land. And they failed the test. Scripture says the Lord forgave them, but they paid dearly for it. You can read the entire account in Numbers 13–14. If only they had realized that relying on God presents the least danger and being self-confident and moving without God brings the greatest danger. God had an army ready to deliver them into the Promised Land.

"Because he himself suffered when he was tempted, he is able to help those who are being tempted" (Hebrews 2:18 NIV).

"Submit yourselves, then, to God. Resist the devil, and he will flee from you. Come near to God and he will come near to you" (James 4:7–8a NIV).

We can face our challenges with confidence when we walk with God. We can persevere through our most difficult seasons with Jesus by our side. He will not lead us in a direction without first preparing the way.

Bumps in Our Journey

Have you had a bump in the road? A trial that shook you to your core? Have things not gone as planned? Maybe you've been tested by fire. Maybe you're in a battle you didn't see coming and you can't see your way out of it.

Bumps can change us.

Consider the woman in the Bible caught in adultery (see John 8:1-11). She didn't plan on being caught, but when the Pharisees showed up, she knew her life would change. In fact, she probably thought her life would end that day.

But that "bump" introduced her to Jesus, who stood beside her, offered no condemnation and told her to sin no more. That one act changed her life.

The bumps I've experienced have changed, shaped and even sharpened me — so much so that I am a different person. When I thought I was done, Jesus picked me up and gave me a firm foundation, hope for a better tomorrow, and the will to keep going.

Jesus stood in the gap for me and remained by my side until I was no longer the same.

Bumps can be used for good.

I encourage you to view your bump in the road differently. Maybe it will project you into a new phase in life. Perhaps it will remind you of what God has already done in your life. Or it could possibly serve as a wake-up call to fulfill the purpose God has for you.

I wish I knew the rest of that woman's story. Did she go back and pick up the pieces? Did she repent from her lifestyle and follow Jesus? Did she tell others of the mercy, grace, forgiveness and new life extended to her?

My nephew and son went back to get that bed frame. It was torn and scarred from the impact and from being dragged across the concrete, but it was still strong enough to do what it was designed to do.

We may not be hauled down a dusty, brick-paved road to a makeshift trial. However, we'll likely be scarred and bruised from the impact of our bump.

Even so, we can still be used for good. With Jesus by our side, we have the strength to do what God designed us to do.

Take that bump — that trial, that test — and let it be used for good.

Listen to the Right Voice

- What step is God asking you to take?
- What giant keeps you from crossing over to the other side?
- What obstacle holds you captive?
- What hurt still grips your heart?

Listen to the One who calls you to follow His direction. With Jesus by your side, you *can* cross over and conquer the giants. You *can* take that step of faith. You *can* overcome that obstacle.

The Source of All Comfort

Could it be that going through difficult times — even if it's our own fault or the consequence of our own sin — teaches us, prepares us or moves us along in our journey?

I could write a book about the many things that happened to my family, particularly financially, in one seven-month period. Not long after we moved into our new home, our 22-year-old truck — parked on the street in front of our house — was hit by another vehicle . . . and totaled. That truck had been the "rite of passage" for my sons as they became first-time drivers. We were about to make that transition for my third and youngest son.

This, along with a host of other repairs and other general issues, sent me wallowing in my misfortune. At one point, my son asked me, "Mom, do you think we're being tested?" I didn't know how to answer except to say, "It sure seems like it."

Instead of going straight to the source of all comfort — to the One who already knew my situation — I turned to earthly comforts. Oh, I cried out to God, but I focused more on complaining to my friends and family. While my friends offered sympathy and comfort, it was God who lifted my head and answered me.

Times like these do, in fact, draw me closer to God. Difficulties often show me that He is near. And in that nearness, peace can be found.

When trials and temptations come, I know I can trust Him, not only because He is God and creator of the universe but also because I can see how He has been with me — by my side — over the weeks, months and years. Through each trial, through each heartbreak, through every decision whether good or bad, He has been there.

We can expect an onslaught from the evil one, especially if we're working to point others to Jesus. He will work with all his might to frustrate us and prevent the work God has for us. We may be quick to glance at temptation and see it only as tiredness, illness or some unmet need.

However, we need to see it as temptation and recognize trials and temptations as planned by Satan himself.

Our story doesn't have to end there. Jesus provides rescue. He watches over us and protects us.

CHAPTER FOUR

God's Protection and Rescue

Quote:

"God does not stop at rescuing us; the purpose of that rescue is to enjoy fellowship with us."

— A. W. Tozer

Scriptures:

"But the Lord has become my fortress, and my God the rock in whom I take refuge" (Psalm 94:22 NIV).

"The LORD himself watches over you! The LORD stands beside you as your protective shade" (Psalm 121:5 NLT).

Song:

"I Just Need U" by TobyMac

I saw it coming but could do nothing about it. On a dark interstate one hour from home, a car suddenly veered toward us. My friend, who was driving, tried to steer us out of the way, but it was a moment too late. The other vehicle made contact and ran us off the road.

The four of us in my car checked on each other, then released a long-held breath. The two in the other vehicle survived the ordeal without injury as well. This may sound bizarre, but I pictured God's angels there between us, softening the blow. Incredibly grateful, we sat in the grassy median watching traffic speeding past.

I didn't know all the behind-the-scenes activity going on as we drove home that night, but I could recognize God's protection. I could trust the strength of God's army. I could know that God is with me and that He sometimes uses misfortune for a greater purpose. Maybe the accident even served as a wake-up call for the person who hit us.

I believe He watched over us and sent an unseen shield to protect us that day.

Beyond the Ordinary Protection

Throughout her life, Rachel has experienced God's protection many times, but two instances stand out as unusual and miraculous. Both times, she ended up outside the window of the car. Both times, someone was there to help instantly but later nowhere to be found.

Growing up, we did not have seat belts and rode up front with our parents in the car. On one occasion, probably when I was close to two years old, I stood on the front bench seat resting my head on my mom's shoulder.

She turned left quickly, which caused me to stumble and fall out of the passenger side window.

Mom was terrified she had run over me. When she got out of the car, an older woman showed up and asked if she could help her. She untied a scarf from her hair and wrapped it around my bleeding head injury.

This woman told my mom she would ride in the car and hold me while Mom drove to the hospital. She walked in with us to the emergency room.

After getting me checked out at the hospital and cleared to go home, my mother asked where the woman who came in with her had gone. She wanted to thank her for her kindness. The hospital staff answered they did not recall a woman with her, that she came in alone with me upon entering the emergency room.

Fifteen years later, I was driving on my own and became distracted while on my way to work. I swerved and quickly reacted to veer back on the road. I jerked the steering wheel too quickly, causing my car to flip. As the car rolled, I apparently fell out the driver's side window and was pushed into a muddy ditch.

I rose up out of the mud like a swamp creature, visibly shaken and crying. My car also had flipped landing right side up, but a metal fence post had gone through my gas tank. Thank God that car didn't explode!

A man on a motorcycle witnessed the accident and stopped to check on me. The next thing I remember was my grandparents driving up to help me.

They recalled that a man called to tell them about the accident and let them know I was okay. He told them exactly where it had happened and that he had already called the police. They asked his name, but he hung up, leaving them confused.

Rachel remembers the man asking if she was okay, but that's all. God protected her that day as well as the accident the day she was two. And I'm sure many times in between and throughout her life. How many times have we had close calls that could have been the Lord's protection?

Recognizing the Protection of God

Once I took my car to a repair shop to get an estimate on some accident damage. Just as I arrived, the alternator belt slipped and the brakes failed.

Questions immediately flooded my mind. What if my brakes had gone out while I was driving? What would I have done? What could have happened?

My next thought was one of awe and gratitude. God had protected me from harm that day and used that situation to encourage and remind me of His presence and protection.

Have you ever felt God's protection? Maybe the way God has shown up for you isn't as dramatic or recognizable as a car flipping or narrowly escaping a disastrous brake failure, but this doesn't mean His protection is absent from our lives. For believers, His presence and protection are constant.

Unwavering Faith

Daniel's story reveals evidence of God's protection and presence. His steadfast faithfulness brought about God's protective hand. The Jewish prophet served King Darius of Babylon and his successors while also remaining true to the God of Israel.

However, after being maliciously accused of breaking the king's law, Daniel was sentenced to spend the night in a den of lions. At daybreak, the king went in haste to the den and cried out in anguish:

"O Daniel, servant of the living God, has your God, whom you serve continually, been able to deliver you from the lions?"

Daniel replied, "O king, live forever! My God sent his angel and shut the lions' mouths, and they have not harmed me, because I was found blameless before him; and also before you, O king. I have done no harm" (Daniel 6:20–22 ESV).

This story of Daniel's faithfulness to the Lord brings several things to light:

- King Darius wanted to see God save Daniel. Verse 16 tells us that he declared to Daniel, "May your God, whom you serve continually, deliver you!" He had watched Daniel and wanted to see what Daniel's God would do.
- Daniel had been captured as a young man at the first siege of Jerusalem, yet he remained faithful despite this adversity. His example shows us how we can remain true to our faith and honor God in all our circumstances.
- Daniel illustrates how to live a holy life. He prayed and gave thanks to his God regardless of the environment around him. The king even recognized him as a man who served his God continually.

Daniel's survival of the lions' den changed King Darius. Verse 25 tells us that he wrote to all the peoples, nations and languages telling them to tremble and fear before the God of Daniel.

Who Fights Your Battles?

This story reminds me of another instance in the Bible highlighting God's protectiveness: God protected Elisha and his servant with an invisible army. Elisha, one of the most well-known prophets of Israel, served in the northern kingdom. He had been anointed by Elijah, a prophet who got to skip death. Elisha watched as God suddenly picked Elijah up in a chariot of fire and took him to Heaven in a whirlwind (see 2 Kings 2:11–12).

Elisha had seen God do amazing things.

Maybe that's why he appeared calm and confident when a powerful detachment of Syrian cavalry and foot soldiers surrounded the city of Dothan, aiming to capture Elisha.

Elisha's servant, however? Not so much. The frightened servant rushed to the prophet and reported what he had seen.

The scriptural account reads:

"When the servant of the man of God rose early in the morning and went out, behold, an army with horses and chariots was all around the city. And the servant said, 'Alas, my master! What shall we do?' He said, 'Do not be afraid, for those who are with us are more than those who are with them.' Then Elisha prayed and said, 'O Lord, please open his eyes that he may see.' So the Lord opened the eyes of the young man, and he saw, and behold, the mountain was full of horses and chariots of fire all around Elisha" (2 Kings 6:15–17 ESV).

There really were more with them than those in that army. Instead of seeing a threat, now Elisha's servant saw the strength and glory of God's army.

I imagine he was never the same again.

With a bold prayer and trust in his Lord, Elisha captured the Syrian army without bloodshed. His successful strategy stopped the raids and brought peace to the land. (See the rest of the chapter for the interesting details.)

Raiding parties were no match for a nation under the Lord's protection. Elisha's servant was reverently awed by the Lord's power, not by the miracles of Elisha.

Thousands of years later, the apostle John reminds us that God's army is still fighting our battles with us:

"You, dear children, are from God and have overcome them, because the one who is in you is greater than the one who is in the world" (1 John 4:4 NIV).

Stand Firm in Faith

An account of King Jehoshaphat in 2 Chronicles reminds us to look to God, not men, and tells us where to place our trust. I love what King Jehoshaphat says when enemy armies are about to attack the Israelites.

"We do not know what to do, but we are looking to you for help" (2 Chronicles 20:12 NLT).

When faced with the news of an impending invasion, Jehoshaphat was alarmed but sought the Lord for guidance.

The Israelites tasted fear. The armies of Ammon, Moab and Mount Seir surrounded the people of Judah and Jerusalem.

Outside of a miracle, they knew they had no hope. In a God-honoring move, King Jehoshaphat admitted his weakness and humbly acknowledged the One who was strong. Their eyes focused on the living God.

We may not be in a physical battle, but our trials can mimic one. We may feel surrounded by the enemy and bound by fear. But fear amplifies the power of the enemy while minimizing the greatness of God.

I love the NIV version of this verse, too.

"We do not know what to do, but our eyes are on you"
(2 Chronicles 20:12 NIV).

Jehoshaphat's answer also speaks for us. No matter the pressure, fix your eyes on Jesus. If walls seem to be closing in or something leads to destruction in your life, remember Jesus stands for you and provides for you.

2 Chronicles 20:17 describes the Spirit of the Lord coming upon one of the men of Judah, Jahaziel. God used Jahaziel to speak to Jehoshaphat. The essence of His message? When facing a battle, He told the people of Judah not to do anything.

"You will not need to fight in this battle. Stand firm, hold your position, and see the salvation of the Lord on your behalf, O Judah and Jerusalem. Do not be afraid and do not be dismayed, tomorrow go out against them and the LORD will be with you" (2 Chronicles 20:17 ESV).

From Fear to Faith

I love the Israelites' response. They praised and sang *before* the LORD delivered them. God caused their enemies to destroy each other. By the time Judah got there, all they needed to do was pick up the spoils — more than they could carry! It took them three days just to collect it all. Don't you love that?

That is who I want by my side.

"At the very moment they began to sing and give praise, the LORD caused the armies of Amman, Moab and Mount Seir to start fighting among themselves" (2 Chronicles 20:22 NLT).

The battle you face today may require you to do something. Or it may not. It might require you to stand still, which sometimes turns out to be the most difficult part. How many times have I forged ahead, not waiting to see what the Lord would do? How many times have you?

I do not know what He has in store for you, but I do know this: With Jesus by our side, we cannot lose. We can rely on our unchanging God to fight and win the battle for us.

God or Coincidence?

When we do not trust God for our protection, we resort to taking control ourselves in an effort to secure our future.

Often, we think of situations like the wrecking of my truck or even the appearance of rescuers after Rachel's accidents as coincidences. What if they're not?

Think about a time you were spared from harm. Maybe you didn't recognize it at the time, but what if you had witnessed God's deliverance?

Trust the strength of God's army.

When was the last time you were amazed at the Lord's resources?

I'm grateful that God protects us and fights our battles even when we are completely unaware.

Remember these two things today: First, as Christians, the One who is in us is greater than the one who is in the world (see 1 John 4:4). Second, although we can't always see it, God is by our side, and we can trust the strength of His army.

I pray God will open our eyes so we can see His glory, His protection and His good work in our lives. But even when we can't see God working, choose to believe He fights for us behind the scenes.

"Be strong and courageous. Do not be frightened, and do not be dismayed, for the LORD your God is with you wherever you go" (Joshua 1:9 ESV).

Trust Jesus for Guidance

Call the name of Jesus often. It doesn't dispatch Him like a genie in a bottle, because He is already there beside us. Instead, it opens our own eyes so we can see and recognize His presence.

Let these promises of the Lord sink in. With all the Israelites' mistakes, their disobedience, and lack of faith, God still rescued them.

"I took you from the pasture, from following the flock, to be ruler over my people Israel. I have been with you wherever you have gone, and I have destroyed all your enemies before you" (1 Chronicles 17:7b–8a CSB).

God still shows up. He still delights in His creation. We have this promise. God rejoices over and delights in us.

"The LORD your God is in your midst, a mighty one who will save; He will rejoice over you with gladness; He will quiet you by

his love. He will exalt over you with loud singing" (Zephaniah 3:17 ESV).

Not only that, but the Lord promises to guide us and bring us peace.

"Because of the tender mercy of our God, by which the rising sun will come to us from heaven to shine on those living in darkness and in the shadow of death, to guide our feet into the path of peace" (Luke 1:78–79 NIV).

Be on the Lookout for God's Guidance

We need to look to Him for our guidance. Let's try to live so that we are always on the lookout for the protection, presence, power and guidance of God. When in times of depression, rejection and loneliness, use those experiences as reminders of God's presence in our lives. The power of those reminders helps us make it through the difficult times and seasons to come.

CHAPTER FIVE

Depression, Rejection and Loneliness

Quote:

"The Holy Spirit brings us consciousness of the actual presence of God, the gifts of divine joy and peace, great and continuing delight in prayer and communion with God."

— A. W. Tozer, Mornings with Tozer, March 19

Scripture:

"And lo, I am with you always, even to the end of the age" (Matthew 28:20b NASB1995).

Song:

"Heaven Help Me" by Zach Williams

A 19-year-old boy took his own life. A son. A brother. A cousin. A friend. Why did he do it? What was the turning point that sent him on that downward spiral to make such a decision? Oh, that I could turn back time so that he could find hope. He would find that he was not alone.

Never Alone

Jesus knows we will go through hard times, but He doesn't want us to go through them alone. He's here for us. He's not surprised by our situation, and He runs to our rescue.

Because God took the Earth that was without form and void, a dark empty mess — chaos — and turned it into light and life, we know He can bring order out of disorder and confusion.

Our lives may feel like chaos at times. Or maybe all the time. But God's word brings life and peace, undoing the chaos and bringing beauty and order.

"For God is not a God of disorder but of peace" (1 Corinthians 14:33 NIV).

You are not alone. God is drawing near even as you fix your eyes on these pages.

God is patient and deliberate. We don't have to tiptoe around Him. He can handle our feelings and emotions, and He understands and cherishes them.

"Pour out your heart like water before the presence of the Lord!" (Lamentations 2:19 ESV).

Living in Survival Mode

Lynne fell to the floor at a boiling point. Anger rose up like a tidal wave, surging before crashing upon the shore.

Her dream of marriage had shattered. Her sense of self-worth had been picked apart. So she sat and yelled at God, wishing she could feel God's closeness again. "Why is this happening? What's next? How do I start over?"

As I attempted to navigate my loss after an abusive and controlling marriage, depression and rejection set in. I reached out, but no one believed me. After four months, I took $500 and left everything I owned.

I wrestled with my ministry after walking through the divorce. I wrestled with my belief in God and who He is. I wrestled with my relationships.

I felt as though God was far away and went weeks without saying a single prayer or reading from the Bible. People ignored me or talked to me like it never happened. One day, I just let it all out and fell to the floor, wishing I could feel God's closeness again.

That's when I kept hearing Psalm 142 in my head. This profound chapter had helped me in many seasons of my life. It had been a favorite scripture through the years.

A spiritual switch flipped in my life.

God's peace washed over me, and I felt a deep sense of God's presence. He reminded me that He was there when it all happened. He would be there going forward and get me through.

Lynne got up from the floor that day certain God was with her and would guide her no matter what came her way. She began to rebuild her life with Jesus by her side. She rekindled her desire to read her Bible and returned to church.

People asked Lynne how she still believed, how she could trust. She used that time to speak truth about God. "Just because God was aware of my situation doesn't mean He inflicted it on me."

God used scripture to remind her of His unwavering love and His constant presence. Lynne now allows God to use this truth and her story to encourage others to apply scriptures to their lives.

Abused and Rejected

The 16th of 18 children, Pearl grew up with a paranoid and schizophrenic father. She, along with her siblings, witnessed her mother endure domestic violence. While her sisters lived with her mother, Pearl and her three brothers grew up under the control of a father who ruled with fear and intimidation.

I never received a hug growing up, was never told "I love you" by my parents. We lived in survival mode, trying not to do anything that would warrant a beating by my father, who became enraged at even minor infractions. There were no birthday parties or outings, no birthday or Christmas gifts.

I experienced rejection for much of my life because of his illness. In my preteen years, my brother sexually molested me. I was given no hugs, no support or counseling — instead, I just witnessed my brother's beating.

The abuse ended when I moved to my mother's home at age 13. I graduated from high school and began attending college. But the emotional damage had been done, leaving scars that could not easily fade.

My rocky upbringing impacted how I saw myself, how I viewed the world and how I managed relationships. While in college, I dated an older man who became violent. Familiar feelings of rejection surfaced — he did not love me enough to treat me like a lady and not a punching bag. So I left.

I eventually began dating again and became pregnant. I graduated college as a single mother with an infant son searching for full-time employment. I faced rejection once again from the baby's father's family, who gave no financial or emotional support. I remained determined to raise my son in a safe, loving environment with the opportunity to gain a good education.

The continued rejection in my life left its mark on my spirit, making me feel like damaged goods.

Even when I met a nice man, I was unable to see him for who he was because of how I saw myself. But he loved me for me. That was a new experience that took some time to accept.

But then, God showed up in an unexpected place. I worked for a probation and parole office and helped direct a project to establish a reentry program called Formerly Incarcerated Person (FIP) for people released from prison. The program helped people reenter and stay in society.

During that time, I met an ex-convict who invited me to attend a "Walk to Emmaus" retreat. That experience led to a turning point in my life. I saw God demonstrate His genuine love, and as a result, I came to know Jesus as my personal Lord and Savior.

Because of Jesus, I learned to forgive. It's not always easy to forgive, but it's harder to deal with the poison of unforgiveness. It's not easy to move forward after a disappointment, but it's harder to stay stuck in anger.

Through her tumultuous upbringing and events in her younger life, Pearl learned three things:

- Even in times of isolation and rejection, she must always strive to treat people the way Jesus treats her.
- Look for opportunities instead of problems. This applies to all life situations — parenting, dating, marriage, work, community and church. Live with a mindset of serving others where they are.
- Accept God's love. The more Pearl understood who she was in Christ and His love for her, the more she could forgive those who harmed and rejected her, even people who had caused her to isolate herself and miss the life God intended for her to have.

Pearl chose to let go of the bitterness, the regret and the remorse. She chose to forgive. Struggles still come, but through her faith and the people God has placed in her life, Pearl lives a healthy and whole life and inspires others to do the same.

Bold Faith

He sat on the dirt road on the outskirts of Jericho. "Have mercy on me!" became his mantra. Tired and alone, he begged. Day in. Day out.

How long had he been on his own? In this condition?

Begging for scraps. Praying for healing. Did he bolster his strength one more time when he heard Jesus was walking his way? Did he gather the resolve for one more shout for mercy?

That shout brought Jesus to a standstill.

"Then they came to Jericho. As Jesus and his disciples, together with a large crowd, were leaving the city, a blind man, Bartimaeus (which means "son of Timaeus"), was sitting by the roadside begging. When he heard that it was Jesus of Nazareth, he began to shout, 'Jesus, Son of David, have mercy on me!'

"Many rebuked him and told him to be quiet, but he shouted all the more, 'Son of David, have mercy on me!'

"Jesus stopped and said, 'Call him.'

"So they called to the blind man, 'Cheer up! On your feet! He's calling you.' Throwing his cloak aside, he jumped to his feet and came to Jesus.

"'What do you want me to do for you?' Jesus asked him.

"The blind man said, 'Rabbi, I want to see.'

"'Go,' said Jesus, 'your faith has healed you.' Immediately he received his sight and followed Jesus along the road" (Mark 10:46–52 NIV).

After Jesus told his disciples to call the man, I love what the disciples announced next.

"Cheer up! On your feet! He's calling you."

The blind man sprung to his feet and came to Jesus.

Jesus knew what was on the man's mind, but he asked.

The blind man spoke boldly. He didn't want to miss his opportunity, so when others tried to silence him, he shouted even more.

His faith healed him that day. He received his sight immediately.

When Jesus Calls

This story reminds me of a conversation I had with a friend who is now with Jesus. It left a lasting impression on me.

As she drove, she envisioned Jesus sitting in the front seat beside her. He asked her these same words. "What can I do for you today?" And she shared her heart's desires.

Could we pause for a moment and call out to Him? He's calling for us, and that fact alone should lighten our load and cheer us up. The call of Jesus is an invitation from the King of the World.

We can rest assured He knows what's on our mind. He knows the longing of our soul.

We can cheer up because the King of the World wants to do something for us.

Our faith plays a role in the outcome.

We need to believe He is who He says he is.

We need to know that He will do what He says He will do.

We need to believe He can heal us.

When we encounter Jesus, we want to follow Him.

I need to be reminded of these words often. When our week brings pain or illness, call out to Jesus. When loneliness or depression sneaks into our day, call out to Jesus. When our faith needs a boost of energy, call out to Jesus.

Be brave. Live boldly.

Be resolved to focus on Him — not our environment or circumstances.

The Bible tells us we *have not* because we *ask not,* and we *have* because we *ask* (see John 4:2–3). Our next move should be to pray until the answer comes. He welcomes our communication with Him.

"Here I am! I stand at the door and knock. If anyone hears my voice and opens the door, I will come in and eat with that person, and they with me" (Revelation 3:20 NIV).

I want my faith to strengthen as I follow Him. I want that for you, too. Today, let's call out boldly, then listen and be encouraged as He calls us to receive the blessings He wants to give us.

Make Room for Interruptions

She was on a routine errand. Trudging to the well to replenish her water supply, she expected nothing out of the ordinary. She could have passed by without a word and ignored His request.

But she didn't. She stopped to listen and was rewarded for it. This woman went to draw water for a stranger, but she received so much more.

Scripture says that because of the woman's excitement over finding the Messiah at the well, she wanted to tell someone. What she did next changed her community. She left to share her discovery with her village, and many of the Samaritans from that town believed in Christ because of this woman's testimony (see John 4:39).

Consider also the apostle Paul. He was on a mission to stamp out Christian influence in the world — until the Lord

Jesus Christ interrupted his journey one fateful day. Paul could have rejected the call, but he didn't. What he did next impacted the world. At once he began to preach in the synagogues that Jesus is the Son of God (see Acts 9:20).

Learn from the woman at the well and the apostle Paul. You may have a busy schedule and no time for interruptions, but that interruption may be the instrument that changes the outlook of your entire day. So avoid automatically discounting it. Jesus invested His life in us. Let's be open to interruptions and invest in others.

Experience God in Your Journey

After reading my story in chapter 1, you know I am no stranger to rejection and loneliness. Since my husband passed away, I've felt alone countless times — at parties, where it seemed everyone had a partner, or even walking out of church with thousands of people.

Jesus is with us in our aloneness. When we experience heartbreak and loss, we can experience God in our grief journey, too. With God's help, we can learn to thrive and live a life of fullness, even in our suffering.

God can enable you to see beyond the pain to the goodness, peace and purpose He offers every day. After all, He remains right by our side.

CHAPTER SIX

Heartbreak and Loss

Quote:

"The promise of God's compassionate presence with us in this world funds our hope. There are many things we don't know, but we know this — we are not alone. And we know this — God comes close, to locate Himself with us in our pain."

— Kristi McLelland, The Gospel on the Ground, pg. 154

Scripture:

"You turned my wailing into dancing; you removed my sackcloth and clothed me with joy, that my heart may sing your praises and not be silent. Lord my God, I will praise you forever" (Psalm 30:11–12 NIV).

Song:

"Scars in Heaven" by Casting Crowns

"Why did God send the ants?" my youngest son asked his brother at the dinner table.

With five-year-old wisdom, my middle son quickly answered, "You know that God can hear you. He can even hear you in Disney World."

In his deep, raspy voice, the younger brother shouted, "God! Why did you send the ants?!"

Oh, to be as bold as a three-year-old.

What question do you want to ask God today? Do you need to cry out in agony? Do you want to shout, demanding an answer?

I spoke with a friend after an unimaginable tragedy and the sudden loss of her 16-year-old nephew. My eyes filled with tears at her statement: "Everyone I love is completely broken." While we spoke on the phone, I could picture the sadness in her eyes as well as the anguish of the others involved — a community staggering to regain its balance.

Another family embarks on a cancer journey, one member soon to begin chemo and surgery. Still another deals with the unexpected loss of a job. A husband and wife struggle to hold their marriage together, while others are making hard decisions for their elderly parents' care.

What do you do when the world around you is off-kilter? When it has lost its balance? When it is shattered in a million pieces and everyone you love is broken?

You cling to Jesus.

I share the ant story not to downplay the severity of loss and pain, but to remind us that God hears not only what comes from our lips but from our hearts as well.

Seek the Lord. He hears. He is present in all of creation, yet also with us in the middle of our own chaos and pain. He gets trauma and grief. He understands hopelessness and anxiety.

Jesus takes our hand and walks beside us. He is trustworthy and He will never fail us. He draws near. We can call on Him with our questions.

Shattered Dreams on a Long, Dark Road

When we learned our unborn daughter had Potter syndrome and would not live once she was born, I felt as though the world had paused and I was watching myself from above. I will never forget walking out of that doctor's office and sitting on the bench outside. As we sat, I cried in my husband's arms.

I cried out to God, too. I knew He could heal her. I never doubted that. Plus, we had countless friends who held us up through prayer. But that was not our story.

We walked through the next months devastated, going through our daily routines in a daze, our hearts numb.

My husband didn't talk much about it. He continued living but with a sense of detachment. Consumed with his own loss, he couldn't offer support that required him to talk. If I needed someone to talk to (and I did), I would have to find someone else.

It was a long, dark road. I cannot even tell you how I made it through that season. But God was with us and walked beside us.

One of the hardest things I can remember during that time was sitting through the Mother's Day church service two weeks after receiving the news, attempting to keep it all together.

One of the most encouraging things I remember happened during a routine dental appointment. My dentist asked how my pregnancy was going, and I told him the news. He stopped right away and gathered his staff around my chair. They all laid hands on me and prayed over me. They interceded for me in a profound and meaningful way. I will never forget that moment and am forever grateful for it.

I saw my dentist at a book signing not long after I released my first book, and I reminded him of that experience. With wet eyes, he told me he remembered it, too.

In that prayer, his boldness spoke to me.

We filled our days with work. Loneliness set in. People didn't know what to say to me, so they avoided me. If they didn't know our situation, they would ask when the baby was due. I had two choices: Lie and act like everything was okay or tell the truth and make them uncomfortable. I did both.

In God's mercy, I went into labor one month early.

Although our baby didn't survive the trauma of the delivery, my nurse took pictures once Ashlynn was born. We have a picture of my husband looking over my shoulder at her in my arms. I remember gazing up at him and seeing that he was about to lose it emotionally. The pain was more than his heart could bear. So I handed her back to the nurse, even though I didn't want to let her go.

Later, I knew I needed to see her again. I told my husband I knew he couldn't, but I needed to. He left the room, and the nurse brought her back. My mom and I were able to inspect her from head to toes. I'm so glad I took those few moments to see my baby — every beautiful inch.

Although he wrestled with his own grief, my husband was a man who got things done: He stepped up when the time came and made the necessary decisions. He became my rock. Though he was way out of his comfort zone, he handled everything. While I recovered at home, he shopped with his mom for burial clothes options and brought them to me so I could choose. He picked out the casket and even took pictures so I would know what the inside looked like.

We grieved the loss of our beautiful baby girl. Of our hopes and dreams for our family. I ached to hold a baby in my arms.

I stayed at home, alone in my grief. Until 9/11. I remember my husband called me on his way to work and told me to turn the television on — two airplanes had crashed into the World Trade Center. After watching the news for two days, I decided it was time for me to be around people again, and I went back to work on September 13, my original due date.

That season nearly broke us. However, we began to grow stronger as Jesus spoke peace into our sorrow, and we began to hope again.

He gave us the strength to take one step in front of the other as we grieved. He brought us through that heart-wrenching and painful time using our friends and church community. And we learned to laugh again . . . to dream again.

The Emotion of Grief

Mary and Martha of John 11 in the Bible provide a glimpse into the human sorrow that surrounds a loved one's death.

After sending a message to Jesus about their brother Lazarus' illness, they expected Him to come see His friend. They simply stated a fact. "Lord, the one you love is sick."

In the accounts of Lazarus, we never hear of him speaking — the Bible doesn't record his words. Martha and Mary had plenty to say, and in some cases, the attitude to back it up.

While Lazarus emerged from the tomb fully alive and well with a second chance at life, the heart of the story belongs to the grieving sisters. They were upset and brokenhearted by Lazarus' death. They felt all the emotions we feel at times of illness and death. A tidal wave of grief washed over them as they struggled with the loss of their brother.

Jesus answered Martha and Mary's implied request that day, just not in the way they expected.

Hope After Grief

God gives us hope after loss. Through long hospital stays or sudden passings, God comforts the downcast. He gives us the stamina to lift one foot in front of the other and strengthens our bonds with family and friends. He encourages us through a friend's visit or a much-needed phone call.

Jesus promises we will see our loved ones again if we have a personal relationship with Him. He promises to prepare a place for us so that someday we will be with Him for eternity. He also prepares us for that place. He's doing the prep work in us now — by leaving us His word so we can know what He's like, by refining us many times through our trials and challenges, and by drawing us to Him through the Holy Spirit, which is His guarantee that we will one day be with Him.

One day His work will be complete, and He'll be ready for us to move in. In the meantime, Jesus promises to be with us and to one day return so that we may be where He is.

I can't even comprehend our joy on the day we get to move into our heavenly rooms. However, surely that moment cannot compare to the joy of seeing Jesus face to face.

"In my Father's house are many rooms; if it were not so, I would have told you. I am going there to prepare a place for you. And if I go and prepare a place for you, I will come back and take you to be with me that you also may be where I am" (John 14:2–3 NIV).

A Hope-Filled Life

A hard winter freeze destroyed my sweet olive trees. Once evergreen, they became leafless and sparse. I wondered if I would ever delight in their scent again.

However, I found a green layer hiding underneath the dry, gray bark. It spoke of beauty to come. Beauty from devastation. This speck of hope, when touched by the sun of spring, will find new life.

While a storm robbed my trees of their leaves and color, I look forward to the day I get to see their beauty once again, inhale their sweet fragrance and rest in their shade.

Does your life sometimes mirror these sweet olive trees? I know mine has at times.

Cold. Hard. Uninviting. Withdrawn and without hope.

But beneath our exterior, we hope for better things to come.

Jesus Christ offers us that hope. He is the lifeblood within us. He brings beauty from our devastation. And he will give us new strength that allows us to grow and flourish.

Be encouraged, my friend. This season of sadness or emptiness will one day blossom into life again. Life that comes from the life-giver Himself.

If you know Him, you know He is faithful. Cling to Him in the good days as well as the not-so-good days.

If you do not yet have a relationship with God and don't know the love of Christ, would you trust Him today? Jesus came to Earth, did what He said He would do, and then paved the way for us to live with Him in eternity. He absorbed our punishment — the punishment we deserve — on the cross that day. He gave us what we could never earn on our own.

His *death* was a gift of *new life* for anyone who will accept it.

Jesus sees great value in you and tenderly calls your name. Receive His gift of salvation by putting your faith in Him.

Receiving His salvation means recognizing you are a sinner, repenting of your sin, confessing with your mouth that Jesus is Lord, and believing in your heart that God raised Him from the dead.

All who receive His salvation are changed by the Holy Spirit and are born again, becoming children of God and receiving eternal life with God.

Alive Again

That olive tree appeared dead. But it would look alive again one day. Thank God He can do the same with us. He can take a life that's broken and without hope and transform it into a vibrant, full life.

The lyrics to the song "Miracle Power" by We the Kingdom express where our hope lies. We may not know what lies ahead, but we can trust the One who creates each day. God is actively involved in the world, not distant or detached.

That is the hope we have in Jesus. We can give Him our burdens. We may not know what's coming, but when we know Him as our personal Lord and Savior, we can have hope. After all, He owns the day.

"Because, if you confess with your mouth that Jesus is Lord and believe in your heart that God raised him from the dead, you will be saved" (Romans 10:9 ESV).

"But those who trust in the LORD will find new strength. They will soar high on wings like eagles" (Isaiah 40:31 NLT).

A God-Guided Life

Because of His ultimate sacrifice, we can trust that He is big enough, strong enough, and cares enough to handle our burdens. Just as God promised Moses His presence would go with him, His presence goes with us, too. Through the rescue. Through the wilderness. In rebellion, in obedience. Through the valley and on the mountain.

Wait for guidance in every step. Trust that Jesus answers prayers.

CHAPTER SEVEN

Answered Prayer

Quote:

"Is prayer your steering wheel or your spare tire?"

— Corrie ten Boom

Scripture:

"The LORD is near to all who call on him, to all who call on him in truth" (Psalm 145:18 NIV).

Song:

"Just Be Held" by Casting Crowns

My son said a bad word in elementary school. He didn't know it was a bad word at the time. But I got the call and took him home. I then headed back to the school to talk with the disciplinarian.

My son sat praying while I was away. He prayed his punishment wouldn't end in a referral that would keep him out of school for a couple of days.

When I returned home to tell him he had been cleared to return to school, he jumped up with excitement.

"That's the first time God has answered a prayer of mine!"

It warmed my heart that he saw God in that situation.

It is a message for all of us. God answers prayers and guides us on our journey.

The Right Time, the Right Decision

Jennifer became a believer at a young age and learned to rely on God's guidance when making big life decisions.

As a young, single mother, she found making those decisions alone frightening and overwhelming. She also called on trusted and wise Christian friends and family to help make the "big" decisions in her life.

Her trust in the Lord was tested at times.

Like many of us, she worried about money and whether her financial needs would be met.

> *When my son was about 13 years old, I was worried about how I was going to pay a specific bill.*
>
> *I spoke of trust often in our home, so he did not question the meeting of that need. In fact, he would remind me of my own words.*
>
> *"I don't know why you always worry about money, Mom. God always takes care of us!"*

I felt peace come over me at that point. He was right! I just needed to hear that from someone else and God spoke to me through a young teenager.

I can't begin to tell how many times I was worried about money, but something always worked itself out. Either I would receive an unexpected check in the mail, or I found something that cost less than planned, or I would come across someone who blessed me with something that made my life a little easier.

In a different season of life many years later, I decided to sell my house and purchase something better suited. It was a big decision, and I planned to wait until my son and daughter-in-law sold their home and relocated for his new job.

I casually commented that I wished I could buy their house. With my son's encouragement, that statement set in motion a series of conversations that led to leaving the house I had lived in for nearly 20 years.

It frightened me to take that step. But God blessed me through it. I sold my house for more than I expected before even listing it.

I started searching for a new-to-me house. I looked at two homes. I dismissed the first option right away because of the kitchen's small size. I love to cook and have lots of cooking things. The kitchen was too small for all my stuff. Or so I thought!

The second house needed some work, but I fell in love with the idea of a project and making that house my own. I prayed continuously about the entire situation. I checked out the house with my mother, her best friend, my friends and my son.

We talked about painting the walls, changing the flooring and even taking down a wall! I couldn't sleep at night because I was thinking about renovations and where to put furniture. I wanted that house.

Even so, I kept telling God, "If this is not the right house for me, make it clear that it is not the right decision." I applied for a loan that would allow me to do all the renovations I wanted to do, fully expecting the process to end there. But I was approved for the loan, and the next step was to get a home inspection. Then I hit a brick wall. That sudden stop turned out to be a blessing in disguise.

I listened to my home inspector and withdrew the offer. That time brought about much stress and anxiety. Partly because the house belonged to friends!

I took a step back and considered the first house again. I shared my concerns about the kitchen with a friend, and she came up with some creative solutions.

After a positive home inspection, I made an offer. The entire process took less than a month. Start to finish! Everything fell into place without any issues. I now have a home that I love in a neighborhood where I have made new friends and strengthened relationships with old friends.

I saw the ease with which everything fell into place as confirmation that God's hand was on this effort from the beginning. When I review that process, I am so glad that I listened to God . . . and to my home inspector!

How often does God use our children to remind us of our own words? It happens to me often.

God blessed Jennifer for her obedience to seek Him in her decision. The process took little time and blessed Jennifer in many ways.

Where Is Our Focus?

Jennifer made God a priority in her decision-making.

Many times, we try to pave our own way instead of focusing on Jesus and allowing Him to work. Instead of inviting Him into our decisions.

When the king of Assyria's field commander camped outside Jerusalem and taunted the people of Judah, they were silent, as commanded by King Hezekiah. After Assyria's attempts at manipulation, Hezekiah's ambassadors came to him with torn clothes and a discouraging message from Assyria.

"As soon as King Hezekiah heard it, he tore his clothes and covered himself with sackcloth and went into the House of the Lord" (2 Kings 19:1 ESV).

After Hezekiah heard the word from Assyria, he went to God. He didn't react to the enemy's threat. In the middle of his despair, he first sought the Lord.

"Hezekiah received the letter from the hand of the messengers and read it; and Hezekiah went up to the house of the LORD and spread it before the LORD. And Hezekiah prayed before the LORD" (2 Kings 19:14–15a ESV).

Praying for Help

So what do we do? How do we respond when we're accused? When we're ridiculed? Or tempted? When we question whether the Lord is enough?

Will we lay it before God and pray for help?

Let's follow Hezekiah's lead and go to God first. Let's place our focus on who God is and His uncontainable power and love.

He knows the way. He owns the road map. He provides the resources, and He cares about the details.

Answers to Your Questions

When Nicodemus questioned Jesus, He confronted him with the truth.

And God's Spirit began to move in Nicodemus. He had questions. Jesus had answers. Jesus spoke life into him.

"Jesus replied, 'Very truly I tell you, no one can see the kingdom of God unless they are born again'" (John 3:3 NIV).

Then Jesus spoke possibly the most well-known scripture in the Bible.

"For God so loved the world that he gave his one and only Son, that whoever believes in him shall not perish but have eternal life" (John 3:16 NIV).

Nicodemus was open to the truth. It seems he had not hardened his heart as some of his fellow Pharisees had.

Did Jesus' words penetrate his heart? Were his doubts replaced by faith? We don't know all of his story, but we do know that later he defended Jesus and assisted Joseph of Arimathea with Jesus' burial. He provided the expensive spices used in preparing Jesus' body, a burial fit for a king. He once approached Jesus under the dark of night. But his actions (and extravagance) in burying Jesus were very much in the public eye.

Something had changed in Nicodemus. When Jesus' closest friends left in fear and deserted Him, Nicodemus did the opposite. He didn't think of his position, his reputation or his wealth before assisting Joseph. He had been transformed and his actions spoke volumes.

Initially, he believed Jesus to be a prophet sent by God even though he knew the stories of old, of a prophesied messiah. He knew the miracles of the Israelites' deliverance during Moses' day. Jesus spoke to Nicodemus about the Israelites' impatience, their plight in the wilderness and the lack of bread or water. The Lord sent venomous snakes that bit them as punishment, and many died. When the people repented and asked Moses to pray to the Lord on their behalf, God instructed Moses to make a pole with a bronze snake at the top to hold up in front of the people. If they looked at the bronze snake, they lived.

Jesus went on to relate this story directly to the saving grace He would provide.

"Just as Moses lifted up the snake in the wilderness, so the Son of Man must be lifted up, that everyone who believes may have eternal life in him" (John 3:14-15 NIV).

The snake on the pole could only save people from physical death. Christ saves us from spiritual death and gives us eternal rescue. Nicodemus knew this story and must have made the connection when he saw Jesus lifted on the cross that day.

Nicodemus came to Jesus as a spiritually blind, prominent religious leader. He left knowing he had encountered the truth.

Do you have questions? Jesus has answers. Through His death and resurrection, He provided our rescue.

Not only is He always by our side, but He speaks to us in all and through all. In salvation. In our daily routine. In sickness. In health. When we need answers.

Living Out Our Faith

Another man in scripture also encourages me to live out my faith more boldly. This man had many reasons to be proud. He had status as an important royal official. He most likely had friends and a loving family. But none of that mattered in this moment. When he heard Jesus was visiting Cana in Galilee, he found himself begging for mercy.

All pride left him as he urged Jesus to go with him to Capernaum to heal his son.

"Once more he visited Cana in Galilee, where he had turned the water into wine. And there was a certain royal official whose son lay sick at Capernaum. When this man heard that Jesus had arrived in Galilee from Judea, he went to him and begged him to come and heal his son, who was close to death.

"'Unless you people see signs and wonders,' Jesus told him, 'you will never believe.'

"The royal official said, 'Sir, come down before my child dies.'

"'Go,' Jesus replied, 'your son will live'" (John 4:46–53 NIV).

The man took Jesus at his word and departed. While he was still on the way, his servants met him with the news that his boy was living. When he inquired when his son got better, they said, "Yesterday, at one in the afternoon, the fever left him."

Then the father realized this was the exact time at which Jesus had said to him, "Your son will live." So he and his whole household believed.

This official believed Jesus before he saw evidence that Jesus had healed his son. He sought Jesus. He listened to Jesus. He believed the words Jesus spoke. He lived out his faith. Then he continued his journey.

Jesus' words say He is with us and that He will never leave or forsake us. We can count on that.

Seek Him.

Listen to Him. We have His word that is filled with instruction and wonderful promises.

Believe Him. Believe in spirit and truth. Do not waver. Continue on the journey He has laid out before you. Call out to Him and see His marvelous works in every detail of your life.

God Is in the Details

I rely on my car's GPS quite often.

My sons and I were on our way home from North Mississippi. This time the GPS left out important details. The route took me through a "shortcut," putting us right in the middle of farm fields.

We ended up on a maze of dirt roads in the Mississippi Delta. By the time we got out, we were at least 15 minutes behind our schedule.

Unlike a GPS, God is perfect and cares about the details. He won't leave them out. He is the ultimate GPS.

In the book of Exodus, He gives very specific information on who was to build the Tabernacle and how, among other instructions.

God Knows You by Name

In Exodus 33:17, God tells Moses, **"I know you by name."**

That might not surprise you since God called him to deliver Israel out of slavery in Egypt. However, Exodus also tells us God also knew Bezalel by name and filled him with the Spirit of God.

"And he has filled him with the Spirit of God, with skill, with intelligence, with knowledge, and with all craftsmanship, to devise artistic designs, to work in gold and silver and bronze, in cutting stones for setting, and in carving wood, for work in every skilled craft" (Exodus 35:31–33 ESV).

The chapter goes on to say God inspired Bezalel to teach others.

God provided the details for the building of His Tabernacle, and He also gave the craftsmen the skills and intelligence to do the work.

God Provides the Road Map

My friend, when God calls us to do something, He also gives us the road map *and* the abilities necessary to complete the assignment or task. Consider what He did for the Israelite craftsmen:

- God stirred the hearts of every craftsman He wanted to do the work.

- He put skill and intelligence into the craftsmen to know how to build the sanctuary exactly like He wanted it.
- He provided them ample resources through the contributions of the people of Israel. The material was sufficient to do all the work and more.

Every detail had been laid out. Every pillar, molding and curtain. Every ring, pole and vessel.

We need not worry about how we will accomplish the work God has called us to do.

Though burdens may arise, He will help us through them, as we continue His work. But when we serve a different master, like the world, fame or approval of others, our burdens become too great.

I tend to rely on myself too much. I get overwhelmed and end up in a maze of uncertainty, the opposite of resting and trusting in Jesus.

> "If my faith, my belief, my confidence are in myself, then they cannot at the same time be resting in God!" (A. W. Tozer, *Mornings with Tozer*, August 30).

I need to remember that He will give me exactly what it takes to get to the end of the path He has laid before me. And He'll do the same for you.

God is in the details.

Let God Be Our Spiritual GPS

God answers and guides us on our journey. We don't need to know what lies ahead. Just go one step at a time and let Him lead. Enjoy His presence and find beauty and joy. We can have joy because He guides us.

Sometimes we fail to recognize God's hand at work because we're deeply involved in our circumstances. But later reflections often reveal how clearly God has worked.

As I thought on this, I also came across scripture that reminded me He didn't start something in me only for me to leave it unfinished.

One of the most familiar verses in scripture, Philippians 1:6, reminds us that God completes what He starts. Jesus didn't do all He's done just to leave us alone. His love is beyond comprehension. His power is uncontainable.

God has a word for us. Set our eyes on Him. Place our focus on Him.

Go to Him. Let God face the world for you.

Sometimes we don't choose to trust God. He answers our prayers, but we can't see them because we're too deep in fear and anxiety. Jesus knows our fears. He remains with us, waiting for us to give them to Him.

CHAPTER EIGHT

Fear and Uncertainty

Quote:

"I learned that courage was not the absence of fear but the triumph over it. The brave man is not he who does not feel afraid, but he who conquers that fear."

— Nelson Mandela

Scripture:

"Do not be afraid, for I have ransomed you. I have called you by name; you are Mine. When you go through deep waters, I will be with you" (Isaiah 43:1b–2a NLT).

Song:

"I Will Carry You" by Ellie Holcomb

The forecast called for fierce winds. I had dropped off my sons with my parents so they could watch them while I was five minutes away at a Bible study. We ended early so everyone could get home before the storm hit. I drove quickly to my parents' house to pick up the boys. They were 11, eight and six years old.

As I parked in their driveway, I saw a tree branch blowing wildly in the wind. I worried it would snap and land on my car. The timing couldn't have been worse. At a young age, my eight-year-old son had become terrified of storms, and we had a 10-minute drive home in wind and rain. I quickly grabbed the boys, essentially throwing them in the car.

Halfway home, I glanced in the back seat and realized my eight-year-old was holding his breath. I told him to breathe. "Take deep breaths and breathe." My oldest quickly answered with his dry wit, "Somebody needs to give him a paper bag."

When we arrived at home, I pulled up the weather app on my phone and showed him the storm on the radar. The worst of the storm had passed while we were driving.

That reassurance helped him move past the fear, accept that he would be okay, and finally settle down.

Two Stories of Faith

Matthew 8 includes two stories of faith (or lack thereof) early in Jesus' ministry. When Jesus entered Capernaum, a centurion sought Him to heal his servant who was paralyzed and suffering at home.

Jesus offered to go to the servant. But the centurion answered there was no need to come but to just say the word, and his servant would be healed (see Matthew 8:5–13).

Amazed, Jesus applauded his faith.

"Truly, I tell you, with no one in Israel have I found such faith" (Matthew 8:10 ESV).

On another day, Jesus and His disciples were in a boat traveling to the other side of the sea. A great storm appeared and a deluge of rain swept down. They didn't need a weather app to watch the storm travel across the radar. They had Jesus. But Jesus slept in the back of the boat. In their fear, the disciples awakened Jesus, asking Him to save them from destruction (see Matthew 8:23–27).

Jesus' reaction?

"Why are you afraid, O you of little faith?" (Matthew 8:26 ESV).

Jesus then got up and rebuked the winds and the sea. And a sense of calm washed over everything.

Jesus could have calmed that first angry wave and stilled the first gust of wind. But because He didn't, look at the lesson they learned. These ordinary men witnessed an extraordinary event that changed their lives and helped them move past their fear. Though the wind calmed, their thoughts were anything but peaceful. They no longer feared the storm. They feared Jesus. Who was this man who controlled the wind and sea? They also experienced awe and a strengthening of their faith. How could they not? After that day, they must have known there was nothing Jesus couldn't do.

With renewed confidence, they then traveled and shared their stories without fear. They taught, preached and healed boldly.

A Season of Fear . . . and Faith

On a hot, humid May afternoon, Mattie answered a heavy knock on her door. Through tears, her husband's coworker relayed the news of the on-the-job accident that changed her life forever.

Her husband, Sonny, worked on a construction crew building the interstate bridge that would cross the Mississippi River from Louisiana to Mississippi.

A cable anchored to a pylon lost its tension, causing the cable to slip and swing through the construction site. It caught two of the crew. Sonny was the lucky one, as the cable hit him across the legs. His friend and coworker lost his life.

This debilitating accident when he was 36 years old landed him in Boston for six months — 1,500 miles away from home. The Catholic hospital near the worksite kept him for a month until he was out of danger. He then left for a Boston hospital and later went to a rehab facility.

Their children were young, so the severity of the devastating situation was lost on them. But not on Mattie.

> *Waves of terror, panic, grief — all the emotions — overwhelmed me while I waited in the hospital. Waiting felt like a lifetime. But through it all, I felt the presence of God with me. I kept reciting Philippians 4:13 daily, trying to stay grounded in my faith.*
>
> *"For I can do everything through Christ, who gives me strength" (Philippians 4:13 NLT).*
>
> *After Sonny suffered a bout of gangrene, his prognosis looked grim. Early on, I got news he might not make it. I was afraid and didn't know what to do. I was a 29-year-old stay-at-home mom. I didn't know how I would feed*

our three kids, all under the age of eight. I worried what was going to happen to us.

My husband did not know the Lord, so while I worried about his life, more importantly, I was anxious about where he would spend eternity.

I waited alone in a room with my fear and anxiety. At some point, a nun from the hospital came in. She told me that my husband was going to be okay.

I never saw that nurse again. But I believed her. In a sense, I gave my fears to the Lord that day. Hope began to take root in me. I felt a sense of calm wash over me and found the courage to keep praying.

I believe an angel visited me that day. We were there for a month and she never returned. God was definitely with me. From the moment I heard the news, He was with me.

Two years later, Mattie's husband gave his life to the Lord. And Mattie lifted her heart in gratitude.

She found the courage to wade through this difficult season, provide the support her husband needed in recovery, and bring their children up to trust God no matter what.

"When anxiety was great within me, your consolation brought me joy" (Psalm 94:19 NIV).

"Cast all your anxiety on Him because He cares for you" (1 Peter 5:7 NIV).

A Bold Move from Fear to Courage

J. R. R. Tolkien once said, "Courage is found in unlikely places."

That's what we find in the story of Esther. Hers was not an army-commander type of courage. Nor one accompanied by physical strength and stamina.

Her courage was quieter — a willingness to risk her life for her people.

After being queen for about three years, she experienced the test of a lifetime. Haman, second-in-command of Susa, the Persian capital, had devised an evil plan to destroy all Jews throughout the kingdom and convinced King Xerxes to sign it into law.

Esther's cousin, Mordecai, challenged her to step in and use her position to change this course of action. A task not easily done, for one was not allowed to knock on the king's door to ask a question.

The law required the king extend an invitation. And 30 days had passed since Esther had been summoned by the king. Did she question her ability to do what Mordecai expected? Did fear strike her heart?

She risked her life for her people. Her response to Mordecai must have been a chilling one.

"When this is done, I will go to the king, even though it is against the law. And if I perish, I perish" (Esther 4:16 NIV).

How do we move from fear to courage?

Several things contributed to her courage and ultimate victory to make such a bold move.

Even before this time, God had prepared Esther for that critical moment in Jewish history.

She was adopted by Mordecai, who treated her like his own daughter. He taught her God was always in control.

She was one of the virgins chosen as a potential queen, winning the favor of Hegai, the king's eunuch and overseer of the king's harem. He even moved Esther and her maids to the best place in the harem.

Esther won the favor of everyone who saw her.

She won the king's favor and approval more than any of the other virgins.

She had an accountability partner in Mordecai, who challenged her to do the right thing.

Esther reported an assassination plot against the king.

Then, before she approached the king about the new law, she called on her people to fast and pray, putting her faith in God first.

After being taken from her cousin to become the possession of a cruel king, Esther could have become bitter. Instead, she demonstrated courage, patience and wisdom. She did this not only in her gracious appeal to the king but through offering a solution that gave the Jews the chance to survive.

And that is the way with us, too. Sometimes our trials springboard us to a place of courage and boldness. Like Esther, God prepares us for these moments through a consistent, everyday walk with Him. Obedience in the "little things" could be just what gets us through that next obstacle.

What Do We Do with the Sting of Pain?

Life is hard. Difficult times happen. Pain *will* come. When it does, do we turn to God or from Him?

You may be thinking, "I do not have the courage of Esther." But consider this. Esther took one step at a time, allowing her trials to shape her into a courageous young woman. She didn't settle for less than God's plan for her. She strove for the best, whether she suffered for it or not.

And we can, too. We can find the courage when courage seems in short supply. We *can* pray boldly and act boldly. We *can* live in victory.

Mattie did. Although a young and fairly new believer, her trust in the Lord brought her through her uncertainty and fear.

Do you have a decision to consider? A plan to implement? How has God prepared you to be bold? Draw upon those experiences that have made you into who you are today and take courage in your moment of decision.

"But as for you, be strong and do not give up, for your work will be rewarded" (2 Chronicles 15:7 NIV).

Fear Talking

What fear holds you captive? The one that steals your peace. Is it a fear of failure lingering in the back of your mind? Do you suffer from a fear of rejection? Does the fear of the unknown keep you from stepping outside of your comfort zone?

God knows our deepest fears, and He wants us to release those to Him so we can experience the joy He has for us. He wants us to be free from the chain of fear wrapped tightly around our hearts.

Strengthen Your Faith

Can you put your fear aside, recognizing that Jesus is in the boat with you and has the power to calm your storm? He knows you. He knows your weaknesses and your fears. Your hopes and dreams.

He is with you when you need healing, courage, confidence or protection from the storm.

Let His presence strengthen your faith and bring you life, hope and power.

Do not fear. He will not fail you.

"Be strong and courageous, and do the work. Don't be afraid or discouraged, for the LORD God, my God, is with you. He will not fail you or forsake you" (1 Chronicles 28:20 NLT).

Out of Egypt

In some of my darkest days, I know God stood beside me. I may not have seen a cloud by day or a fire by night, but I know that His presence was with me then and is with me still.

As the Israelites were slaves in Egypt, I was a slave to fear and uncertainty.

The Lord brought the Israelites out of Egypt with His strong hand. God brought me out of the darkness in my life that resulted from loss and grief.

The Lord did miraculous signs and wonders before the Israelites' eyes. God brought people into my life, scriptures into my path and songs into my heart that have spoken, encouraged and lifted me from a deep darkness that was my life for a time.

The Lord brought the Israelites out of Egypt to give them the land He had promised. The Lord gave me peace, joy and hope and brought me back into the land of the living.

They were no longer slaves. I was no longer a slave to my grief. With Jesus' sacrificial death and resurrection, we are no longer slaves. He has broken our chains, and we are to live free in the presence of the living God.

Times of fear and uncertainty draw me closer to God. Difficulties often spotlight His nearness. It is in that nearness that we can find peace.

Like King David, when fear and disappointment come, I know I can trust Him, not only because He is God and creator of the universe, but because I can see how He has been with me — by my side — over the weeks, months and years. Through each trial, through each heartbreak, through every decision whether good or bad, He remains beside me.

Do you know who to turn to? Whom to cry out to? Who is sure to answer? No matter what comes, Jesus Christ is there every step of the way.

"Praise be to the God and Father of our Lord Jesus Christ, the Father of compassion and the God of all comfort, who comforts us in all our troubles, so that we can comfort those in any trouble with the comfort we ourselves receive from God" (2 Corinthians 1:3–4 NIV).

There is a reason the Bible tells us not to be afraid. Bible scholars debate how many times "fear not" shows up there, but we know it's a lot.

God knows our deepest fears. He knows us. He knows when we've lost our way. He knows when we've wandered off the path He has for us.

No matter what we've done or what's been done to us, He knows and He cares.

He offers forgiveness and encourages us to forgive others.

CHAPTER NINE

Sin and Forgiveness

Quotes:

"Forgiveness is an act of the will, and the will can function regardless of the temperature of the heart."

— Corrie ten Boom

"Man has two great spiritual needs. One is for forgiveness. The other is for goodness."

— Billy Graham

"There is no greater joy that can be compared to that which God gives when He forgives us, cleanses us, restores and saves us, and assures us that the gift of God is indeed eternal life, to as many as will believe."

— A. W. Tozer, Mornings with Tozer, August 22

Scripture:

"In Your presence is fullness of joy; at Your right hand there are pleasures forever more" (Psalm 16:11 NKJV).

Song:

"God, Turn It Around" by Jon Reddick

S he had committed the unthinkable, giving in to earthly desires. In the process, she destroyed her own small family and another marriage as well.

Seven years later, she found Jesus and surrendered her life to Him. Only God could have given her the courage to do what came next:

She called me. The unfamiliar voice sought forgiveness for her part in breaking up my marriage.

Stunned by her confession, I could honestly assure her that she had been forgiven years before, and I was truly glad she had found Christ. Only God could have given me the strength to forgive and move on with my life.

Forgiven and Changed

Forgiveness. Proof God can make something good out of a really terrible time. Because of forgiveness, God changed me. Because of forgiveness, God changed her. Neither of us was the same person we'd been.

She found Jesus. He forgave her and gave her the courage to follow Him, to confess and seek forgiveness.

That's what God does with betrayal. He pardons and allows a way for restoration and forgiveness. And He calls us to forgive and allow that person to earn our trust once more.

God Changed Everything

Laurie spent 214 days in and out of several hospitals. At one point, her family received news she would not survive. But while stuck in a hospital during the COVID-19 pandemic without family and distractions, she encountered God. And that changed everything. Her newfound trust in the Lord gave her the courage to forgive and find joy and love again. It gave her the confidence to turn away from lies and hate to truth and the goodness of God.

I asked Jesus into my heart during a revival at my church at age eight. As my brother, who is 15 months older, was about to make his profession of faith, I also felt that "tugging" or "fast heartbeat" people speak of. I certainly did not want him to leave me behind, so I stepped out and made my profession of faith beside him.

I have never questioned my faith, but I definitely have not walked with God many times throughout my life.

I was fortunate to be raised in a loving, Christian home. I did not know what it was like to not go to Sunday school and church.

During my youth, I was involved in church. As a young adult, I worked with the youth, and as a young married adult, I took my kids to church. Was I always faithful during this time? I can tell you I was not. . . . I know now my life was so much harder, unhappier, and more stressful when I was not walking with Jesus. Life is so much easier with Him.

At 14, I began dating what I would call my childhood sweetheart. He was 17. My parents did not approve because of the age difference. I later discovered my parents were wiser than I gave them credit for, but I did not want wisdom from them at the time. I pushed them away. I only went to them when I was in need or in crisis mode. Does that sound familiar? Just what I did and still do at times with God, my heavenly Father.

Oh, how we create our own mess! The wonderful childhood sweetheart I knew I was supposed to marry was a serial cheater. He cheated when we dated, and we dated for almost nine years. After 15 unfaithful years of marriage, I filed for divorce.

I had so much hate toward him and toward the women he saw during our marriage, it consumed me. I was miserable during most of my marriage and continued to be miserable after our divorce.

Why was I miserable? I finally got out of the thing that was making me miserable. I continued to carry that hate inside me for another 20 years. Twenty wasted years! I hated my ex-husband and all of the affairs. I wanted everyone to know what a rotten husband he was.

My hate affected everything in my life. Relationships, motivation, energy, finances. I had no joy in my life. I lived life a miserable person.

I prayed over the years asking God to take my misery from me, to change me and bless me, but I would not let Him have it. I hung on to it. I listened to the lies of the devil. The devil lies!

"The thief comes only to steal and kill and destroy; I have come that they may have life, and have it to the full" (John 10:10 NIV).

I became very sick during the COVID-19 pandemic. As one of the first COVID patients in our area, I went in and out of several hospitals for a combined total of 214 days. At one point, hospital staff told my family I would not survive. While I recovered, I had severe malnutrition, severe muscle atrophy, and severe physical difficulties. I needed extensive physical therapy, occupational therapy, and speech therapy, both inpatient and outpatient.

God began to work a miracle while I was in the hospital. He convinced me to contact my ex-husband and tell him I forgave him and I loved him. Never in the 20 years after my divorce had I considered doing that. No way! Why would I do that after he destroyed my life?

Lying in a hospital bed brings perspective. I had nowhere to go. I was stuck in the hospital where no friends or family could visit. I had no distractions; it was just me and God. I did not want God's wisdom, just as I hadn't wanted my parents' wisdom as a teenager. However, I knew the time had come for me to make a decision and then be faithful and follow through.

I called my ex-husband from my hospital bed and left a blubbering, crying voice message. I do not remember all the words I said. He didn't return my call. But God changed me. It was the most wonderful thing I can honestly say I have ever experienced. At that very moment, my life as I had known it was gone.

I had joy again. I had love again. I had a desire to live and thrive and help others at that very moment. It might sound strange, but it was true!

"He gives strength to the weary and increases the power of the weak. Even youths grow tired and weary, and young men stumble and fall; but those who hope in the Lord will renew their strength. They will soar on wings like eagles; they will run and not grow weary, they will walk and not be faint" (Isaiah 40:29–31 NIV).

For those that lived through it, the pandemic was probably the worst experience we ever encountered. So many friends and family died due to COVID or its complications. I could have been one of those people. God spared me. He gave me more than I had before.

All I had to do was confess, ask for forgiveness, then turn from my ways. Why was something so easy so hard?

I had not been able to work since getting sick, but three months after my experience with God I went back to work, first in a wheelchair, then with a walker and eventually on my own two feet again.

I could share many stories of the blessings I continue to receive from God. He truly is my Savior in more ways than one. I will forever worship Him; I will continue to seek His guidance in the ways I can help others and bring those who are lost to Him. I have such joy in my life now.

His blessings were there all along, but before this life change, I chose to put myself before Him. When you walk with Him, spend time with Him, and spend time in His word, He will reveal and provide everything you need!

As Laurie lay in the hospital bed, she watched the video stream of the Sunday service at her church. A sense of awe and gratitude swept over her as her church family — specifically her pastor — prayed for her health. Even when her family was told to expect the worst, they prayed. And prayed. And prayed.

Humbled by the support of her church family, and with Jesus by her side, she regained the will to live. To work again. To laugh again. To forgive. And to find joy again.

Her world changed that day. She obeyed God's voice and experienced His presence in that room. The Holy Spirit spoke to her and called her to a life of wholeness and joy.

Laurie's healing was twofold during that season. First, from the devastation of COVID and near death. Second, from the devastation of years of betrayal followed by years of bitterness and misery. With that healing came the desire to live, thrive and help others.

I love this description of peace Kristi McLelland gives on page 31 of her book *The Gospel on the Ground*:

Our peace, our *shalom,* is connected to a person, the living God. *Shalom* comes to us through meaningful connection to God. The violence of sin in our hearts and lives and minds disrupts our connection to God. Sin breaks the harmony we have with God and ruins our *shalom,* our peace. Repentance of our sins allows us to reconnect with God and get back on the path of life He's laid out for us.

I believe Laurie experienced *shalom* that day — a place of wholeness, flourishing, harmony and delight. She experienced that meaningful connection with God.

Rescue

The dust swirled as her hands hit the ground. The shuffle of feet sounded around her. Then came the accusations.

Caught in adultery, the scribes and the Pharisees brought her to Jesus to test Him. She awaited the sting of the stones that would crush her and seal her fate.

She was guilty. She knew it. Her accusers knew it. She had been caught in the act and there was no way out.

Did panic set in? Or was she resigned to her punishment of death? Were her eyes locked on Jesus? Or cast down to the ground?

The dust settled and she focused on a hand. Then that hand reached down and wrote in the sand. She dared to glance toward her accusers. One by one, they left.

No one hurled stones her way.

Jesus had her back. He did not condemn her; He rescued her. His words only directed her to go and sin no more (see John 8:1-11).

One Pair of Hands

Written and recorded by Carroll Roberson in 1971, the song "One Pair of Hands" encourages us to put our faith in Jesus. Its lyrics tell us God formed creation with one pair of hands. Jesus healed the sick, raised the dead and fed thousands with one pair of hands.

Like the adulterous woman, we all have sinned. Maybe it's obvious to those around us. Maybe not. Maybe our sin is a lack of faith. Regardless, we all sin.

Consider Peter's short stint of walking on water. He demonstrated great faith when stepping out of the boat to get to Jesus. Bold was his middle name.

But when he began to sink, his confidence faltered and fear gripped him. Once locked on Jesus, his eyes shifted to the wind around him. He began to feel the weight of the water as it soaked into his clothes. He needed a rescue.

In the next moment, a hand reached down and rescued Peter from the shadowy depths (see Matthew 14:22-33).

The Bible speaks of many more rescues at Jesus' hands.

- One pair of hands cleansed a leper.
- One pair of hands broke a loaf of bread, placing the pieces in baskets to nourish the crowd.
- One pair of hands took saliva and dirt and placed mud over the eyes of a man born blind. And gave him sight.
- One pair of hands held babies and children.
- One pair of hands raised a girl to life.
- One pair of hands washed the feet of His closest friends, even His betrayer.
- One pair of hands was extended and nailed to a cross. Arms stretched in agony secured our hope and sealed our fate . . . if we only believe and receive.

The Price Paid

Have you been desperate for a rescue like Laurie was? Do you need to forgive? Do you need to receive forgiveness? Restoration? Salvation?

Jesus has already paid the price. His hands have already done the deed, reaching out to us.

Let the goodness and love of our Lord Jesus Christ wash over you today.

Seek Him and put your faith in the one pair of hands.

"Do not be afraid, for I have ransomed you. I have called you by name; you are mine. When you go through deep waters, I will be with you" (Isaiah 43:1b–2a NLT).

Martha and Peter

Martha made a mistake. She could see it now, but in the moment, not so much. In her quest to make everything perfect and presentable for her visitors, Martha almost missed it. Time with Jesus. Time to soak in what He had to say. Time to learn from His wisdom.

The rooster crowed, and Peter's heart sank. Regret must have poured over him like a heavy fog. How could he have done the very thing he swore he would never do? And especially to Jesus? He had vowed he would lay down his life for Jesus. But he *had* done it. On that fateful evening, Peter denied he knew Him.

The look on Jesus' face must have been fixed in his mind.

Lord of the Second Chance

What did Jesus do? He forgave Martha. He forgave Peter and gave him a higher calling. While scripture doesn't tell us that Jesus brought up Peter's betrayal again, it does say that Jesus gave him another chance to stand up for Him. He knew Peter's heart and told him to feed his sheep. Jesus trusted Peter with those He loved.

He used Peter to build His church.

Other Bible characters come to mind — Jonah, David and Paul, to name a few. They all picked themselves back up and honored God with their lives.

Sometimes it's hard to hand out second chances. But isn't that what Jesus does for us? Let's learn from Jesus' response to Peter and forgive.

We may not think the "small" sins we commit hurt anyone else, but they usually do. As followers of Christ, going in the opposite direction from what God tells us to do betrays the one who loves us unconditionally.

If you don't yet know Christ, salvation is that second chance from God. He made the provisions for our sins. God is all-powerful, all-knowing, holy, infinite, yet He made a way for His people to draw near.

God's love seeks us out and draws us in — no matter what we do or what sin we commit. Sin is sin. It still has to be paid for. But God in His mercy made a way for our sins to be covered.

Move Forward in Faith

Have you been there? When shame washed over you because of something you declared or did? I have. And it's not pretty.

How do we get past the guilt and shame? Past our own human failure?

We move forward by embracing God's love and faithfulness. We may have been wrong, but Jesus makes it right through His forgiveness.

Even in Israel's sin and the countless times they disobeyed God, He still rescued. He still loved them and wanted them to draw close. He went to great lengths to demonstrate His love.

As humans, we fail. But maybe we need to examine our human failure against the setting of God's faithfulness.

When we fail, He is still faithful.

Sometimes we find ourselves in a place of disillusionment and discouragement and think we're past help from God. But that's not truth. Whether we fail or whether our discouragement is a result of someone else's sin or neglect, Jesus reigns and He is faithful.

CHAPTER TEN

Disillusionment and Discouragement

Quotes:

"The Christian life is not a constant high. I have my moments of deep discouragement. I have to go to God in prayer with tears in my eyes, and say, 'O God, forgive me,' or 'Help me.'"
— Billy Graham

"Disappointment is inevitable. But to become discouraged, there's a choice I make. God would never discourage me. He would always point me to Himself to trust Him. Therefore, my discouragement is from Satan. As you go through the emotions that we have, hostility is not from God, bitterness, unforgiveness, all of these are attacks from Satan."
— Charles Stanley

Scripture:

"So that I may make there an altar to the God who answers me in the day of my distress and has been with me wherever I have gone" (Genesis 35:3 ESV).

Song:

"Honestly, We Just Need Jesus" by Terrian

M y books fell off the delivery truck.

I could write a complete page of issues, problems and just strange things that surfaced while preparing to launch my first book, a book about finding joy amid pain and grief. That joy comes through a relationship with Jesus.

I had ordered books to have on hand for the upcoming launch event. They were late.

One day a friend called to tell me someone from a few streets over found my book in the road. One lone book.

I had already received a box that was partially open on one end with books missing, so I could only assume that box's contents somehow fell from the truck.

As issues surfaced, I felt beaten down and battered, like someone intended to discourage and hinder me from completing the book project.

Used for Good

Satan himself is the father of lies and has a multitude of ways to influence our thought processes. Words of discouragement. Words to hinder us from completing what God has called us to do. From the beginning of my book-writing adventure, I stopped and started many times, questioning if I was even doing what God was asking me to do.

And then, two weeks before the book release date, my books fell off the truck. Not one, but a second box arrived a couple of days later — repackaged. All the contents inside were battered, smudged and swollen from water damage.

Stand Strong and Press On

In the end, what was meant to discourage, God used for good.

That neighbor who found my book researched and found me, too. Before she did, she read the book. And then she hand-delivered it to my door with words of encouragement that blessed me and gave me new strength to stand strong and press on.

Should you find yourself discouraged when you're trying to live out God's purpose for you, remember this story. And let it encourage you to keep moving forward in whatever God has called you to do.

And while you're at it, thank Jesus for the people He places in your life to encourage you and when needed, even to hold you up.

Let God use for good what Satan wants to use for evil.

"You intended to harm me, but God intended it for good to accomplish what is now being done, the saving of many lives" (Genesis 50:20 NIV).

A Hidden Past Revealed

Carol sat on her sofa with her husband's locked briefcase. An uneasy feeling welled in the pit of her stomach. Something was amiss; she sensed it.

Married for just three months after a whirlwind romance, her husband frequently traveled and never left the briefcase at home. The sleek black briefcase now challenged Carol's curiosity. But nothing prepared her for what she found inside.

The revelation of her husband's hidden past sent a chilling realization down Carol's spine. A flood of emotions overwhelmed her as she grappled with the shocking truth within the confines of that now-opened briefcase.

He was the Controller at my company and new to town when we met. Highly protective, he put me on a pedestal and poured out luxury with expensive gifts, trips, a new car and more. What more could a woman ask for? I initially loved it, but as an independent woman, I had begun to feel controlled.

On this day, my husband had to go out of town for business, leaving me home alone. As I cleaned our beautiful apartment, I noticed his briefcase in the closet. A possession he was never without.

Thoughts flurried through my mind. Although I loved not having to worry about bills or anything else, my suspicions arose with some inconsistencies he had told me, but I only wanted to see the good and would quickly dismiss any uneasiness I had.

However, now determined to unveil the briefcase's secrets, I began experimenting with different combinations, starting with the basics — birthdays and our anniversary, but the mechanism remained stubbornly closed.

As frustration crept in, I hesitantly entered 123, and to my surprise, the left side of the briefcase yielded. Encouraged, I tried 456 next, but it remained sealed. In a moment of intuition, I entered 321 on the other side, and with an audible click, the right side popped open.

A mix of trepidation and anticipation overcame me as I began to explore the contents. Among the unexpected letters, overdue bills and other documents lay divorce papers, letters from his ex-wives and more concerningly, probation papers from the state where he had once been incarcerated.

Stunned and scared, I called my brother to come. I needed support, advice, and a way out of this revelation that had shattered the illusion of our happy marriage. Along with my dad, we packed my belongings, preparing to leave the life I thought I knew behind.

Just as we were leaving, my husband called. As I began asking questions, the anger in his voice was clear. He had no concern for my feelings. Instead, he was furious that I had dared to open the briefcase and unearth the skeletons in his closet.

He bellowed over the phone. "Why did you open that?" His anger escalated with each passing second. "You had no right to invade my privacy!"

In utter shock, I wept. "I had every right to know who I married. You lied to me about everything. How could you do this?"

He only continued to yell, curse and berate me, revealing his true self in a shocking and frightening way.

The man I thought I knew was no longer on the other end of the phone. Instead, an angry stranger responded — a side I had never experienced before. Fear took over as I realized the horror of the situation.

The days, weeks and months that followed were like something from a movie, but I now know that God was with me the whole time. I leaned on my family and my church for strength, finding solace in prayer and seeking guidance from my pastor. With a heavy heart, I shared the painful truth about the deceit that had been woven into the fabric of my short-lived marriage. The pastor had performed our wedding ceremony and felt a sense of obligation and protection.

As I distanced myself from the environment of deception, my pastor connected me with a network of individuals who could help me navigate the stormy waters ahead. Among them was a Christian FBI agent, who assured me that justice would be served, and he pledged his commitment to ensuring my safety.

My pastor went above and beyond to support me, even offering me his parking place at church every Sunday. This gesture became especially meaningful after I discovered my wedding pictures torn up and plastered all over my car one Sunday.

Not only that, but my estranged husband frequently drove past my parents' home at all hours, causing distress. Police surveillance was established at both my parents' house and during my church visits each Sunday, placing security at all doors as my pastor had identified his behaviors as pathological and unpredictable.

The unwavering support from my pastor and the added security measures played a crucial role in helping me navigate through the turbulent times.

During this time, I discovered an unexpected support system within my church community. Friends and family rallied around me, offering prayer as well as emotional and practical support. With their help, I found a new place to live and began the process of rebuilding my life.

As the weeks turned into months, the legal proceedings progressed, and I found healing in my newfound independence. I was told my ex-husband had returned to his hometown during this time, so I had begun feeling safe. However just as I began to feel comfortable again, I saw *my ex-husband slowly driving through the parking lot of the restaurant a friend and I had just visited.*

He just wanted me to know that he was still around — that he controlled me. And though this startled and shook me, I had a strong network to lean on and God to protect me.

At first, Carol wasn't sure what gave her that sense that something wasn't right but later realized God protected her that day.

Through the fear, anxiety and disillusionment, His divine presence gave Carol a sense of comfort.

The hand of God showed up in the people He strategically placed in her path: a pastor to offer spiritual guidance, law enforcement professionals committed to their faith, counselors and a supportive community that became a lifeline during her darkest days.

Slowly but surely, she emerged stronger, resilient, and with a renewed sense of purpose.

In the end, justice prevailed, and Carol's ex-husband faced the legal consequences of his actions. She discovered that this wasn't his first con, but hopefully, with these consequences, it would be his last.

Carol's story became a testament to the strength found in faith, community, and the unwavering belief that even in the face of adversity, God provides a path forward.

"And no wonder, for Satan himself masquerades as an angel of light. It is not surprising, then, if his servants also masquerade as servants of righteousness. Their end will be what their actions deserve" (2 Corinthians 11:14–15 NIV).

Finding God

A. W. Tozer once said, "Brain power is not the means by which we find God! It is in our dependence on God that we see Him. He graciously and in love revealed Himself to us."

Maybe it's in our desperation that we sense the presence of the Holy Spirit.

Saul Found God

Consider the apostle Paul. Before he was an apostle, destroying Christians consumed him. He went to great lengths to drag them out of their houses and commit them to prison. On one occasion on his way to Damascus, Paul, then Saul — the accuser and one with power and control — lost all control and found himself to be the helpless one (see Acts 9).

After a bright light blinded him, Saul became desperate. In that moment, he found Jesus. One of the men he traveled with led him by hand to Damascus. For three days, he waited without sight, food or drink.

Totally dependent on God, Saul was rescued by one of the very people he came to persecute. God ordained his disciple Ananias to restore Saul's vision.

According to scripture, after a discussion with the Lord, Ananias obeyed and laid hands on Saul.

Two things happened. First, Saul regained his sight. Second, he was filled with the Holy Spirit.

In that unforgettable event, Saul found God.

Jesus didn't fear Saul's sin. Instead, He took his darkness, miraculously changed him and welcomed him into the kingdom. Saul still had power, but this time he went out with the power of the Holy Spirit to bring light to the world.

"All of you, clothe yourselves with humility toward one another, because, 'God opposes the proud but shows favor to the humble'" (1 Peter 5:5 NIV).

The Cry of Our Hearts

Times of disillusionment and discouragement will come. We may feel like life is overwhelming and spiraling out of control.

If we're grounded in our faith, we weather these days. When discouragement comes, we can take time with those close to us and invest in them. We can be more intentional about our relationships and stop fueling the unhealthy ones as well as end any negative self-talk.

We can invest in those who encourage and lift us up instead of those who weigh us down. We can align ourselves with people who support us, encourage us and are bold enough to speak truth into our lives.

I talked with a friend about not feeling good about my appearance, letting myself go physically. I got to a point where I couldn't stand to look at myself in the mirror. She quickly reminded me that was the enemy whispering lies.

Let's avoid listening to the lies and turn our hearts toward our God who sees us and listens.

He knows our hearts and responds accordingly.

What is the cry of your heart today? Do you need to turn away from sin or seek the Lord in humility? Does sadness or disappointment keep you in bondage? Does the pressure you face keep you from living a life pleasing to the Lord?

Take time today to humble your heart and hear from God. Hand over your discouragement to Him and let the living God use for good what was intended for your harm.

Above all, we can trust and obey the One who knows and sees us best, the One who lifts us up, the One who provides and cares for us. In this we find rest.

CHAPTER ELEVEN

Obedience

Quote:

"God is God. Because He is God, He is worthy of my trust and obedience. I will find rest nowhere but in His holy will that is unspeakably beyond my largest notions of what He is up to."

— *Elisabeth Elliott*

Scripture:

"Through him we received grace and apostleship to call all the Gentiles to the obedience that comes from faith for his name's sake" (Romans 1:5 NIV).

Song:

"Abide" by Aaron Williams

Christy and her husband knew God was leading them and so were preparing to go back to a country to work and serve. They had a deep love for the people there and a desire to see them learn the love and salvation of God.

However, a big challenge stood before them like a mountain against the sky. Selling their house. They had tried for months with no serious interest. No offers. Few appointments.

What should they do? They knew God had given them this assignment. But when? At first, they waited for the house to sell before buying flight tickets. Then in a step of obedience in faith, Christy bought the tickets that would take them halfway around the globe. And God flung open every door they had been waiting on.

Multiple offers received. Inspections completed. Possessions either sold or packed up. Kids settled in their colleges.

This encouraging story reminds me of a hymn we sang at church in my younger years, "Trust and Obey."

> *"When we walk with the Lord in the light of his word,*
> *what a glory he sheds on our way!*
> *When we do his good will, he abides with us still,*
> *and with all who will trust and obey.*
> *Trust and obey, for there's no other way*
> *to be happy in Jesus, but to trust and obey."*

These words, penned by John Sammis more than 100 years ago, still resonate today.

The story of the song has been handed down through the years, telling of a new Christian rising to speak during a time of testimony at a Dwight L. Moody revival in 1886. He said, *"I'm not quite sure — but I am going to trust, and I am going to obey."*

Have you been called to do something far out of your comfort zone? When we walk with the Lord, trusting and obeying, we know His voice. We can move forward in confidence because we know His call. We can live in peace because His presence remains with us.

Calm Against an Oncoming Trial

When Leesa walked from the school gym to the classroom next door, she had no idea the situation she would soon encounter. Although she was robbed at gunpoint, she held no fear because God was with her.

She volunteered to oversee the hospitality room that provided meals and snacks for referees, coaches and school administration at basketball tournaments, something she had done for the prior nine years.

She dashed over early so she could review her Sunday school lesson for the next day. As soon as she sat down, she believes God gave her a "heads-up."

As I sat down and gathered my papers, I had the thought, "You're going to be robbed here by yourself." It was an overwhelming feeling — not a casual thought. It's like I knew it would happen.

In all the years working in that room, I had never had that thought before. But with it, two masked 15- and 16-year-old boys immediately burst into the room. They snatched my purse and put a gun to my head. I grabbed the hand that held the gun and said, "That's not a real gun."

Turns out, it was a real gun. He shrugged me off, and both boys ran away.

> *I taught a children's class at the time, and the memory verse for the next day was "Be not afraid."*
>
> *I believe God told me I was about to be robbed, preparing me for the encounter. Because of this, I was not surprised and I never felt fear.*
>
> *I'm probably a little more suspicious of people now, but that day, I was not afraid. I know it was God giving me that sense of calm.*
>
> *My husband and son were supposed to be out of town that night but decided to wait a day. Although I had planned to be at home by myself, they were there with me.*

God was beside Leesa that day. Only God could have given her the impression she would be robbed before it happened. As a result, she stayed calm and didn't panic. Maybe it was God's way of taking the shock out of it.

Thankfully, they didn't hurt her and were caught later. The identifier? The authorities found her pink headphones in one of the robber's pockets.

Because of her daily obedience, Leesa was in tune with God's prompting.

A Daily Walk with God

Walking daily with God, studying scripture and praying deepens our relationship with Him. These disciplines attune us to His presence in our lives, empowering us to recognize His hand in our circumstances. They open the door for us to hear from God, especially when we're approached by something frightening.

Many walked with God in the scriptures. Enoch stands out for having lived in a wicked age yet still living a godly life.

He had such a personal relationship that God decided one day Enoch should be with Him. He transferred him from this life to his eternal life, sparing him from death (see Genesis 5:24). Enoch was walking on Earth with God one moment, and the next moment, he was in God's presence. I wonder what it must feel like for God to be that pleased.

"By faith Enoch was taken from this life, so that he did not experience death; 'He could not be found, because God had taken him away.' For before he was taken, he was commended as one who pleased God" (Hebrews 11:5 NIV).

Enoch demonstrated that we can live a godly life even in an environment of disbelief, moral corruption and rejection of truth.

As we live out a close personal relationship with God, our faith strengthens and empowers us to walk in the power of the Holy Spirit.

We can also learn from Abraham's trust in God's guidance and timing. He knew God, who had made him the promise he would become a father in his old age, was faithful.

According to the book of Romans, Abraham never wavered in believing God's promise. In fact, his faith grew stronger as he gave glory to God.

Don't miss this. As his faith grew stronger, Abraham brought glory to God. The reverse is also true. As we praise God, our faith will increase (see Romans 4:20).

As I have called out to God for strength, I have grown closer to Him. A consistent daily following of God exercises our faith, tests our faith and strengthens us. This lays a foundation upon which we can live out our faith with greater confidence.

God of Possible

"How foolish," I thought as I read Zechariah's response to the angel Gabriel's news. An angel of the Lord had appeared in front of him, and he asked, "How can I be sure of this?"

In his defense, the Bible says that he and his wife Elizabeth were righteous before God (see Luke 1:5–7). In his mind, they were too old. In that moment, he focused on his earthly limitations over what God said He would do.

I can imagine Gabriel's indignation when he declared, "I am Gabriel. I stand in the presence of God, and I have been sent to speak to you and to tell you this good news" (see Luke 1:19).

Speechless

The result? Zechariah was not able to speak again until that child was born.

God put an angel in front of Zechariah. An angel who had just stood in the presence of Almighty God.

How many times have I questioned God's word to me? I may not have seen an angel standing before me, but God's word is clear.

In contrast, Elizabeth didn't hear Gabriel speak but she believed him and gave God the credit.

"'The Lord has done this for me,' she said. 'In these days he has shown his favor and taken away my disgrace among the people'" (Luke 1:25 NIV).

Blessed

Six months later and about 100 miles north in Nazareth, Gabriel showed up on another mission. This time to Elizabeth's relative, a young virgin named Mary. At a young age, Mary walked with God.

Mary's response? Not "How can this be?" but "How will this be?" A few moments later, she demonstrates her faith when she answers, "I am the Lord's servant. May it be to me as you have said." No human reasoning. No asking for a sign. Just, let it be done.

When Mary later visited Elizabeth, Elizabeth summed it up perfectly.

"Blessed is she who has believed that the Lord would fulfill his promises to her!" (Luke 1:45 NIV).

Wow. These two stories teach us what it's like to just trust and obey — no questioning God's announcements. No assumptions. It will be what the Lord says it will be. And know the good that comes to us is the Lord's doing. That's walking with God.

So, the next time I question something God tells me, I'm going to think of Zechariah and Mary.

One old. One young.

One mature. One inexperienced.

One who'd likely seen God work many times.

Both knew the scriptures.

One led by human reasoning. One spirit-led.

One who saw through a "How *can* this be?" lens. One who saw through a "Let it be as you say" lens.

I hope that we, too, can see through Mary's lens and respond accordingly. Because nothing — regardless of age or physical condition — is impossible with God.

Joy and Peace Follow Obedience

When we obey, joy and peace follow.

Obedience demonstrates our love for God. It gives us life and brings glory to Him. It brings about the right response for our good. It aligns us with His will, allowing us to live out our created purpose.

Obedience helps us experience and understand God's love more deeply. It is a natural way to express our love back to Him.

Obedience leads to spiritual growth and maturity. It provides a way to draw closer to God and better understand His heart and desire for our lives. Practicing obedience in small things builds a foundation for when challenges arise.

Obedience fosters greater trust. As we obey, we develop a deeper understanding of God's character and learn to trust Him more fully.

The Unlikeliest of People

God works through broken people — even the unlikeliest of people. We only have to obey, and He will invite us into His presence.

Moses had a rough start. Taken from his home at a young age, he was raised in the home of a wicked, harsh man who eventually sought to kill him.

Moses murdered someone and tried to hide it, but God still chose him to do His work.

In a burning bush, God tells Moses he's the man to rescue His people.

Even though God chose him, Moses balked.

"But Moses said to God, 'Who am I that I should go to Pharoah and bring the Israelites out of Egypt?' And God said, 'I will be with you. And this will be the sign to you that it is I who have sent you: when you have brought the people out of Egypt, you will worship God on this mountain'" (Exodus 3:11–12 NIV).

After a question-and-answer session with God, Moses offered excuses to escape responsibility. God assured him He would teach Moses what to do and gave him his brother Aaron to speak to the people instead of him. Even after God answered all his concerns, Moses still did not want to obey and trust God. He even asked God to send someone else. Finally, he reluctantly obeyed.

God had a message for Moses to deliver, and despite Moses' hesitations, God still chose him to rescue His people.

From taking life to leading the path to freedom; from forging ahead on his own to following God's detailed direction, Moses implemented God's plan to free His people from their bonds in Egypt.

Trust and Obey

My friend, God chooses us, too. We have been given the greatest news ever known to man. Jesus Christ came to Earth in the form of a baby. God with human skin. But let's not miss the second part of this greatest news. Jesus came so he could make the ultimate sacrifice to save the world. And God has chosen us to share this good news!

How do we respond? Are we full of wonder at what was done for us? Do we enjoy God's blessings of people, experiences and things, only to go back to our daily routine?

Or do we respond and obey? Like the shepherds, do we share the good news? Do we go to where the Holy Spirit leads us? For me, I have found that I need to be obedient to what God already has stated before He reveals something new. I believe that one step of obedience at a time opens the door for God to speak more.

Step by Step

I think we can learn from the shepherds visited by the angels at Christ's birth.

- They stopped what they were doing, obeyed and went to see Jesus.
- They returned to their fields glorifying and praising God for all they had heard and seen.

Today, we too can act upon the word of God.

- Stop what we're doing and recognize the splendor of that event 2,000 years ago. Keep the awe and reverence of that moment in our hearts and minds and glorify Him.
- Recognize the gifts He gives us every day.
- Follow in obedience — one simple step at a time.

When we obey and seek Jesus, we can't help but return glorifying and praising Him.

"And the shepherds returned glorifying and praising God for all they had heard and seen, as it had been told them" (Luke 2:20 ESV).

Obedience is not just following the rules. It's embracing our created purpose, deepening our relationship with God and experiencing the fullness of life He intends for us.

"Trust and obey, for there's no other way to be happy in Jesus, but to trust and obey."

No matter the circumstances we are placed in — big or small — God's word is clear. He wants us to trust . . . and obey. Whether it's sickness, suffering or difficulties, a daily walk with God will keep us on the right track, instilling a sense of purpose as well as direction for our lives.

CHAPTER TWELVE

Physical Suffering and Disease

Quote:

"My scars I wear proudly, I want you to see. They are only life lessons that no longer bleed."

— April Peerless

Scripture:

"You turned my wailing into dancing; you removed my sackcloth and clothed me with joy, that my heart may sing your praises and not be silent. LORD, my God, I will praise you forever" (Psalm 30:11–12 NIV).

Song:

"Need You Now (How Many Times)" by Plumb

One day, my 91-year-old dad took off on his scooter to the local grocery store about half a mile from my parents' house. Take a mental picture of this and let yourself smile.

Why was he going to the store? Because he needed his dizziness medication to be picked up, and my mom wasn't home at the time.

So . . . a man battling dizziness who can barely see rode his scooter beside a busy street. He was on a mission to get the needed meds. It's a wonder he made it there at all, as he's been known to run off the curb before getting to the end of the ramp! God must have been protecting him.

Desperate for His Touch

Think for a moment of the story written 2,000 years ago of a woman risking everything to seek healing from Jesus. When she heard Jesus was nearby, she tore through the crowds — on a mission — to get healing from the bleeding she'd suffered for 12 years! She had spent all she had on physicians, but not one was able to help her. She only touched the fringe of Jesus' garment and was instantly healed.

"And a woman was there who had been subject to bleeding for twelve years, but no one could heal her. She came up behind him and touched the edge of his cloak, and immediately her bleeding stopped.

"'Who touched me?' Jesus asked.

"When they all denied it, Peter said, 'Master, the people are crowding and pressing against you.'

"But Jesus said, 'Someone touched me; I know that power has gone out from me.'

"Then the woman, seeing that she could not go unnoticed, came trembling and fell at his feet. In the presence of all the people, she told why she had touched him and how she had been instantly healed. Then he said to her, 'Daughter, your faith has healed you. Go in peace'" (Luke 8:43–48 NIV).

Surely many types of people were in the crowd that day. With determination, she ran past the onlookers — those who were just there to observe. She ran past those with casual curiosity as well as those seeking to find fault.

But this woman was not there to satisfy curiosity or pass judgment. She was there for a life change; she knew where to get it, and that's what she received.

A Driving Force

I want to be that driven to get to Jesus.

The woman plunged into the crowd, found Him, touched the hem of Jesus' clothing, and received the blessing — the healing — she sought. In that moment, she felt His power heal and change her. And He felt that same power leave Him.

Do we seek Him like that? He isn't hiding. He's right here with us, pursuing us. He wants to bless us, and He wants us to know how much He loves us.

After my dad's escapade, I gently scolded him. "Now you can't ride down to the store like that. It's not safe." He said he wouldn't do it again. But with a look of mischief on his face, he added, "Unless I need something."

Let's be driven by a need to get to Jesus. Let's stay focused as we run past the many distractions that demand our attention and steer us astray.

Seek Him. Know Him. Be changed by Him.

"You will seek me and find me when you seek me with all your heart" (Jeremiah 29:13 NIV).

The Power of Choices

Life didn't turn out how Cary had imagined. He found himself at a crossroads after a simple procedure to remove a cancerous brain tumor with an awake craniotomy.

Yes, that's right. He was sedated but awake enough to respond to the surgeon's questions and directions. His treatment consisted of an interdisciplinary combination of surgery, radiation and chemotherapy, considered to be the "gold standard" for the safe removal of low-grade, slow-growing oligodendrogliomas.

During surgery, Cary's right motor strip was compromised. His story reminds us of the impact our choices have on our lives. What could have turned him into a bitter, angry and resentful man propelled him to trust God in and through all circumstances.

> *I suspected something was awry the morning following surgery when my left hand, arm and leg felt as if they were being poked with a hundred pins and needles.*
>
> *When the surgeon checked in during his morning rounds, I shared my symptoms with him. Though it was his duty to oversee my course of care until I was discharged, I never saw the surgeon again. He checked out.*

I was not aware that he had caused permanent injury until 17 months after the surgery, when the chairperson of the hospital's system informed me.

Up till then, I had been referred to nearly 175 physicians, specialists and therapists, all of whom I assumed were moving me closer to recovery, though I didn't notice any significant improvements.

The result? I am permanently disabled without the use of my left hand, arm and leg.

After that, I explored legal options, only to learn that my doctors and other health care workers were shielded from legal action as state employees.

The entire experience, from diagnosis to nearly five years after surgery, has been fraught with breaches of best medical and ethical practices. My numerous requests to meet with the appropriate administrative and clinical staff, as well as the surgeon who performed the procedure, were ignored by hospital administrators.

I was essentially blocked from getting answers . . . and closure.

Years later, the Patient Relations department invited me to submit a list of the greatest concerns related to this surgery. I submitted 16, none of which I was told was inappropriate.

A month later, my wife and I met with a Patient Relations representative and the head of Patient Satisfaction in the Emergency Services. Despite having no neurology credentials, the head of Patient Satisfaction acted as a surrogate for the doctor who performed the surgery.

Instead of presenting all my concerns, I was allowed to ask only one question: Why did the surgeon fail to immediately acknowledge that the surgery had failed and that he had caused permanent damage during the procedure?

I would describe both representatives' approach to answering our questions as sandbagging.

Patient Relations denied my request to resume this meeting to include the surgeon.

I felt abandoned. From frontline caregivers to everyone downstream, there were countless breaches of best practices, which I have documented in great detail.

At first, my unanswered questions consumed and defined me. But then I began to see my life as a journey of faith and growth.

Eventually, I realized I faced two choices: blame my situation on the surgeon and wallow in self-pity and bitterness, or place my trust in God, accept His will and maintain a positive attitude. With God's grace, I chose to follow His lead to move forward.

I now close each day with this version of the Serenity Prayer, a prayer that supplies great peace to me:

"God, grant me the courage and strength to change the things I can; grant me Your peace and comfort in accepting the things I cannot change; and please Father God, grant me the wisdom to know the difference."

What do you do when your way of life is suddenly ripped from your control? How do you overcome such personal devastation and disappointment?

Cary's story is heart-wrenching, filled with challenges that test the limits of human endurance and spirit. He didn't find answers to his questions. He found something more: God's grace.

Because God was with him, Cary could accept God's plan — whatever that might be. His journey is far from over. He has adjusted to his situation through God's grace and the loving support of his wife.

Cary learned that wherever the journey leads, God guides. His choice to trust God has not only influenced his own life but also those around him.

Embracing Scars

My son experienced a once-in-a-lifetime adventure with a few other high school boys. As they reached the summit of a 12,000-foot mountain in Colorado, they celebrated their achievement with excitement and singing.

That exhilaration prompted them to dip themselves in the icy cold stream alongside their campsite. The upside? The thrill of the experience and the joy of their accomplishment. The downside? My son slipped on a tree lodged four feet above the water. As he fell, a branch cut his thigh. He proudly showed me the three-inch mark.

I told him putting vitamin E on it might keep it from scarring. To my surprise, he preferred the scar. It represented a badge of honor — a reminder of his mountaintop experience. "Every time I see it, I'll remember that day."

What Our Scars Tell Us

Physical scars tell the story of the body's natural healing process. They can take up to 12–18 months after an injury or surgery to heal and fade. But emotional scars seem to hang on for much longer, like an old habit that's hard to break.

Yet, they too serve as a reminder. God impressed upon me the significance of our emotional scars. While we may not like the disappointment, the heartache, the trial, the grief or the pain that caused the scar, that scar represents a memory or a season in our lives.

While our inner wounds remind us of a difficult time in our lives, they can also point us to Jesus and His work through that trial. They can remind us of a fearful season as well as God's protection through it. Scars may remind us of a time of our faith*less*ness, but they can also demonstrate God's faith*ful*ness. They can remind us of a time of suffering but also God's love that got us through it.

Maybe like Cary, you have physical scars reminding you of some trauma in your life. Or maybe they're internal, hidden safely inside so no one will know. Has an unkind word left you with a scar? Or have you suffered from a disease that hinders and impacts your future? Maybe you experienced an unimaginable sorrow or a betrayal from someone you loved and trusted.

What Our Scars Teach Us

Scars serve as powerful reminders of our experiences in life and the lessons we learned from them. God sees them all and He's working in them. That doesn't mean we bypass the pain, but that we sense the presence of God through it, of the healing He provides in it. In those moments, we can see He was with us all along.

"The Lord replied, 'My Presence will go with you, and I will give you rest'" (Exodus 33:14 NIV).

Crack in the Concrete

I confidently walked to my parents' carport door — something I've done thousands of times.

However, this time a small crack in the concrete sent me flying. It was a leap I had not intended to take. In that split second, I thought, "This is not going to end well."

After my knees, elbow and hip hit the hard surface, I decided to lie there for a bit before attempting to move. I'm not even sure which area hit first, but they all hurt. I'm pretty sure I landed six feet from that crack.

Have you been there? Confident and sure of yourself. On a mission. Then, something stops you in your tracks. Out of nowhere, you're hit with devastating news. Your plans crushed. Faith shattered.

Or maybe you've nailed down your schedule for the day, and you're eager to check things off your to-do list. Then, one small crack takes you in a completely different direction. Or maybe you feel confident about yourself until a sliver of doubt lets in all kinds of negative thoughts.

A Bold Mission

Those cracks in our lives can take on many forms.

I imagine Jairus, a ruler in the synagogue, never thought he'd see his young daughter at the point of death. But when we find him in scripture, he was on a mission to find hope and healing.

We don't know all the details, but here's what we do know — his confidence was in Jesus.

Mark 5:21–43 tells us in desperation he broke through a great crowd by the sea to beg Jesus to heal her. He demonstrated great faith, saying, "Come and lay your hands on her that she may be made well and live."

In his wilderness season, Jairus cried out to the only one who could save her.

"Then one of the synagogue leaders, named Jairus, came, and when he saw Jesus, he fell at his feet. He pleaded earnestly with him, 'My little daughter is dying. Please come and put your hands on her so that she will be healed and live.' So Jesus went with him.

"While Jesus was still speaking, some people came from the house of Jairus, the synagogue leader. 'Your daughter is dead,' they said. 'Why bother the teacher anymore?'

"Overhearing what they said, Jesus told him, 'Don't be afraid; just believe.'

"He did not let anyone follow him except Peter, James and John the brother of James. When they came to the home of the synagogue leader, Jesus saw a commotion, with people crying and wailing loudly. He went in and said to them, 'Why all this commotion and wailing? The child is not dead but asleep.' But they laughed at him.

"After he put them all out, he took the child's father and mother and the disciples who were with him, and went in where the child was. He took her by the hand and said to her, 'Talitha koum!' (which means, 'Little girl, I say to you, get up!'). Immediately the girl stood up and began to walk around (she was 12 years old). At this they were completely astonished. He gave strict orders not to let anyone know about this, and told them to give her something to eat" (Mark 5:22–24, 35–43 NIV).

Jairus did not know what Jesus would do that day, but he put his faith and trust in Him.

However, as Jesus went toward Jairus' home, the worst happened. Someone from his house came with the devastating news — his daughter had died.

In that moment, did Jairus' mind spring from hope to despair? Did the news stop him in his tracks? Did it paralyze him with fear?

We don't know, but Jesus overheard those who came with the news and confided to Jairus, "Do not fear. Only believe."

Jairus got to see the miracle-working power of Jesus. As did many others that day by the sea and in Jairus' home.

Battle Scars

I have a few scars from that fall at my parents' house, but I did recover. And thank goodness I can laugh about it.

Sometimes I even think I need a keeper.

Wait.

I do have one, and He's right by my side when I fall. When I doubt. When I miss the mark. When life doesn't turn out how I planned it.

These "cracks" have also taught me that you can recover from the twists and turns of life. You can recover from pain and loss to live an abundant life of joy that is grounded in the Lord Jesus Christ.

No matter what happens in our lives, we have one constant: Jesus Christ is the truth, and through Him, we can not only survive what's going on in our lives, but we can also learn to thrive again.

"You turned my wailing into dancing; you removed my sackcloth and clothed me with joy, that my heart may sing

your praises and not be silent. LORD, my God, I will praise you forever" (Psalm 30:11–12 NIV).

In His Time

Are you on a mission to receive healing from Jesus?

Be patient with yourself. Let God's healing take place in your life in His way, in His time. When your scar reminds you of that difficult season, remember the lessons that have shaped you and remember your God who remained by your side.

Sometimes God's healing comes in the form of the people He puts in our lives. He often uses friendships and community to provide the healing or the resources we need.

CHAPTER THIRTEEN

Friendship and Community

Quotes:

"As iron sharpens iron, so a friend sharpens a friend."

— King Solomon

"Friendship is a chain of gold
Shaped in God's all perfect mold.
Each link a smile, a laugh, a tear
A grip of the hand, a word of cheer
Steadfast as the ages roll
Binding closer soul to soul
No matter how far or heavy the load
Sweet is the journey on friendship's road."

— Anonymous

Scripture:

"A friend is always loyal and a brother is born to help in time of need" (Proverbs 17:17 NLT).

Song:

"Tear off the Roof" by Brandon Lake

W hat do you do when a friend is suffering?
Job 2:12 tells us what Job's three friends did.

"When they saw him from a distance, they could hardly recognize him; they began to weep aloud, and they tore their robes and sprinkled dust on their heads. Then they sat on the ground with him for seven days and seven nights. No one said a word to him, because they saw how great his suffering was" (Job 2:12-13 NIV).

You may remember that later they had plenty to say, but at this time, they got it right. They didn't offer their opinions or overused platitudes. They sat with him. They were present.

When Words Are Few

Although my time of intense suffering is long past, anniversaries, special occasions and sometimes random days still get to me. I voiced the upcoming anniversary of my husband's death to the ladies in my Bible study group one night. During the prayer, a friend beside me leaned over and put her arm around me. No words were needed.

On another occasion, a friend visited in my hospital room after the birth — and death — of our infant daughter. Later, she returned with a pair of socks because I had mentioned my feet were cold. Another friend sent me a box of thoughtful scriptures and gifts to open each day for an entire month.

Actions Speak Louder

Actions like these mean the most. Many times, words fall short. It's the simple act of service, the expression of love, the comforting touch that carries deep meaning. Maybe a simple hug is your gift to others. My sister gives great hugs. When she hugs you, no doubt about it, you know she cares.

We all have need of giving and receiving such actions. Pain and suffering surround us. They seem to be the constant in our world today. You probably know someone suffering right now.

If God has prompted you to do something, do it.

When words are few and you don't know how to respond, let your actions speak what words cannot say.

God Goes Before Us

As Blake sat in a patient room at Ochsner Medical Center in New Orleans waiting to be evaluated as a living donor, he received news that turned his family's life around. He knew this day would come eventually but never had he dreamed it would arrive this soon.

In the middle of securing their son's place as a potential liver donor recipient, watching him face a six-hour transplant surgery, helping him recover for weeks away from home — while also experiencing an overwhelming outpouring of love from their community — Blake and his wife Kelli were reminded that God goes before us.

> *We learned our son had liver disease at nine weeks old. He underwent two surgeries: one at nine weeks and then a second a year later.*
>
> *Over the last couple of years, we had noticed his labored breathing. We found out he had developed hepatopulmonary syndrome. Because of that, he was listed as a potential liver recipient.*
>
> *But I was also already in New Orleans being evaluated to be a living donor. The day of my consultation the doctor called with news that astounded us.*

The doctor talked. But Kelli and I didn't hear a word he said. The news was too overwhelming. Too incredible to believe. Our son, now 11 years old, had had liver disease his entire life. Yet, we were told they may have found a donor. Here I was about to be tested to be a living donor, and just in time, they found another candidate. Could this really be happening this quickly? We had assumed we had much more time.

After a few more calls to get a final confirmation, we got the answer. We're doing this.

Kelli's mom had been taking care of our kids for us. There was no time to travel five hours to bring the news to our son personally, so we made a FaceTime call to tell him and help him process the information. Our parents and kids packed within minutes and began the drive to meet us.

We stayed up all night, and by 11 a.m. the doctor began surgery. Then the wait began. Surgery took six hours, but we had to wait for nine to see him.

The part of that day that stands out the most was pre-op. That's when our emotions ran wild. My parents, mother-in-law, our daughter and friends stood together with us. We prayed. We cried. We felt an overwhelming sense of gratitude. It was intense, heart-pounding.

The waiting room full of friends and family impacted us in a profound way. In one day, I shifted gears from being alone in a room undergoing donor testing to experiencing a rich sense of community surrounding us.

God used our community in many other ways, too. From the moment we found out our son would have surgery, people began to send money and food gift cards. My Venmo notifications chimed constantly for 10 days *as financial gifts flowed into my bank account! But God didn't stop there. A total stranger offered a fully stocked apartment to use for the weeks we would be in the city. This gift covered the entire cost.*

I have always said we know God provides because He has taken care of us up until now. And I know He's not going to stop. This experience didn't change that. We had to trust God, however He worked it out.

But I had never seen Him work this way before. It was like God had said, "I'm going to heal your son, going to feed you and give you housing." We didn't have time to worry about it.

God went before us. Literally.

And He went fast. We still have so many emotions. It was a good thing we had to wear masks around our son for those first days after the surgery. I cried every time I saw him, and the mask covered up most of my red, watery nose.

Life still has its challenges. We're not close to normal. It will take some time to be with friends or be part of a crowd, but we are grateful for every step of the way.

My friend texted me one of the most meaningful messages. It came while sitting in the apartment after we were discharged, restless to be back at home. This friend knew what it was like to spend weeks at a time in a hospital room. "As crazy as this sounds, enjoy it. Most likely you will never have to be in the hospital so long again. Try to make good use of the time. Use it as a break and devote it to spending time with your son."

I took that advice and didn't wish that season away. That time was precious, and it allowed me to put everything else aside and be present and thankful in the moment.

Those weeks were fast and furious for Blake and Kelli and their family. They never had time to process all that was taking place. Things moved at lightning speed. They were unsure of what was going to happen, how long it would take or where they would stay. But God knew.

God went before them. He healed. He provided for them abundantly. He blessed them through friends and community.

Answer the Call

"Is your mom okay?" my friend across the table asked, alerting me to my mom's condition. Sitting beside her, I checked and immediately caught her as she began to fall. Holding her up, my friend on the other side and I talked to her frantically to keep her conscious as we waited for an ambulance to arrive.

A woman saw our distress from across the restaurant and wove her way quietly over. "May I pray for her?" We welcomed her whispered interruption. She prayed and we prayed along.

Though her exact words escape me, I won't forget her calming presence. My mom slowly became more alert. Thank God. She doesn't remember much from the experience, just an awareness of the EMT and us talking to her toward the end.

We didn't know it at the time, but my mom's blood pressure had dropped dangerously low due to an issue with her medicine. I thank the Lord for His protection and for sending a believer who demonstrated compassion and a willingness to stand in the gap while we waited.

Courage to Step Out

Today's world often demonstrates the opposite of this compassion and sensitivity. Many would observe but not take the step to help. This visitor stepped out with courage — away from her own dining experience and priorities that day — to pray over a stranger.

Our encounter reminds me of the parable of the Good Samaritan in Luke 10:25–31.

The Samaritan came upon a traveler left half dead on the road to Jericho. He lifted his battered and bruised body, bandaged his wounds, carried him to an inn and took care of his needs. Other people's opinions didn't matter to him. He answered the call to lend a hand and do what needed to be done.

Our fellow diner could not help us physically, but she gave what she could. She lifted my mom to the Father, her words comforting our souls.

I'm sure I thanked her — but I hope she knows how much we appreciate her demonstration of love and care.

Is God calling you to stand in the gap for someone? Do you know somebody who needs comfort? A bandage? An encouraging word? Or a financial gift to help them get by?

"For I was hungry and you gave me something to eat, I was thirsty and you gave me something to drink, I was a stranger and you invited me in, I needed clothes and you clothed me, I was sick and you looked after me, I was in prison and you came to visit me" (Matthew 25:35–36 NIV).

Answer the call. Who knows what God will do through you?

Sometimes that call means a pep talk and attitude adjustment.

Attitude Adjustment

At the whack of the tennis ball against the net, our hearts sank. This match determined whether my son and his tennis partner made it to the next level — state — and they had just lost the first set.

The second set was closer. They pulled ahead, then tied and eventually won the set in a tiebreaker, which meant another tiebreaker was needed to determine the winner of the match.

I cannot tell you how intense that match was. My son, usually upbeat and positive, was down in the dumps. His partner answered the call to reach out to him and had to talk him off the loser's ledge, so to speak. And he succeeded! With a changed mindset and sheer determination, they won.

A positive attitude — being willing to do your best no matter the outcome — reveals much. So, when you see someone being down, maybe God is calling you to remind them of the power of an optimistic spirit, the power of taking action.

Saint Augustine once stated, "Pray as though everything depended on God. Work as though everything depended on you." The boys were working. The parents were praying. There were even a couple of Hail Marys happening on the sidelines, too.

Are you pulled in other directions, sometimes even to a dark place? Sometimes to defeat? And sometimes to another vice?

A changed attitude can launch us back into a life of victory.

Consider Esther's Story

When Mordecai refused to bow down and worship a government official, he sealed his fate and that of the Jews in every province. He went into the city wailing loudly and bitterly.

This caused his loving cousin, Queen Esther, great distress. Mordecai sent word urging her to go to the king and beg for mercy for her people.

Her initial attitude was that it couldn't be done. Just approaching the king was illegal and grounds for execution. Unless the king held out his scepter, she would be put to death.

Mordecai answered the call and encouraged her — helping her focus on her task — with these words:

"And who knows but that you have come to your royal position for such a time as this" (Esther 4:14 NIV).

Then Esther changed her mindset and got to work. She did what it took to save her people. Her profound statement, "If I perish, I perish," spoke clearly to the Jews in that day and serves to encourage us today.

Embracing Great Faith

I love the story of the friends who refused to take no for an answer when trying to get their paralyzed friend to Jesus. Even though the crowd in the room kept them from getting him through the door, their sheer determination found an unusual, bold way to place him right in front of Jesus (see Luke 5:17-26).

They had a "nothing could stop us" attitude.

They found a way around the crowd, carried their friend on his mat to the roof, tore off part of it and then lowered his paralyzed body right into a crowded room.

What was he thinking as he was being lowered? I think he didn't care how they did it. He just wanted to get to Jesus.

He embraced a great faith. His friends demonstrated great faith and went to great lengths to get him in front of Jesus.

Their boldness rewarded them with a life-changing experience. Their faith was strengthened because of the power in Jesus' presence.

Our Greatest Need

Do you have an opportunity to be a friend like that? One who will leave no stone unturned to help someone else? Let's strive to be a friend who will go to great lengths for someone in need.

Be present physically and emotionally. Sometimes the greatest need is simply spending time together and listening. Checking in with a friend who is hurting or suffering, along with offering practical help when needed, shows we care and are thinking about them.

The greatest need our friends often have — whether they realize it or not — is to glimpse Jesus through our actions and support. I have some greatly cherished friends in my life. But our closest friends cannot always be physically present. Jesus can. No one has ever cared for me like Jesus. He's always there, offering unconditional love and care.

God sometimes uses the kindness of others and the support of community to provide for us. I have experienced this in my life. His provision always meets our needs, working through people, miracles and even the mundane.

CHAPTER FOURTEEN

Provision

Quotes:

"I have a great need for Christ: I have a great Christ for my need."

— Charles Spurgeon

"A daily portion is really all we need. We do not need tomorrow's supply, for that day has not yet dawned, and its needs are still unborn."

— Charles Spurgeon

Scripture:

"Wait on the Lord; be of good courage, and He shall strengthen your heart; wait, I say, on the Lord!" (Psalm 27:14 NKJV).

Songs:

"There Was Jesus" by Zach Williams and Dolly Parton

"My Father Has It" by Landon Wolfe

I swerved slightly into the other lane as I rounded a curve. It wasn't a big deal, except my son's exaggerated reaction would convince you otherwise. "Jesus take the wheel!"

Talk about a flair for the dramatic!

Oh, but that statement brings much meaning.

I often have seesaw emotions. One minute, I'm giving my problem or need to God. The next, I'm taking back control as if I know what's best. My human nature wants to forge ahead and set my own direction, not let go and wait for God to step in.

What about you? Does He have the wheel of your life? Or are you gripping it with white knuckles?

Miracles and the Mundane

God works in the miracles and the mundane. He's always there.

Overwhelmed and stressed to the max, Jennifer needed God to intervene, or her son's college attendance would end in financial hardship. After his first year, she received a letter: His financial aid had been cut. She was in desperate need.

> *When my son was choosing colleges, I told him a set amount I could pay each year. I had agreed to pay more the first year to give him more time to save. I also completed a special circumstances application because my income was literally half of the prior year's due to my husband's death.*
>
> *But after that first year, the financial aid was reduced, and we had to cover an additional $8,000 on top of the $4,000 he was already paying.*
>
> *I completed the special circumstances application again, praying they would honor the original amount since my projected income was the same as the year before. I waited with an anxious heart.*

For several weeks, I prayed for God's favor on our financial situation.

When the new numbers came out, we saw that God had enormously blessed him. Not only did they reinstate the prior amount, but they gave him an extra $5,000. Seriously! An $8K swing!

Jennifer prayed for God to supply and then waited. God answered. Her son only had to pay the same amount as the prior year, with Jennifer paying $5,000 less!

God blessed Jennifer and used the waiting time to teach her and strengthen her faith.

Waiting Well

In American society and culture, waiting doesn't make the list of our strengths. But waiting patiently has its benefits. Sometimes the wait makes us realize we don't want the desired outcome after all. Sometimes the wait brings us blessings and shows us part of God's plan.

A Plan to Wait

God promised the shepherd David he would be Israel's next king. God had a plan. But that plan required David to wait.

As a fugitive, David and his "band of brothers" camped out in a cave while King Saul and his army searched for them to kill him.

Not knowing David's location, Saul one day showed up in the very same cave David and his crew hid. Saul stood at the entrance unaware. David's men encouraged him to take Saul's life, but he refused. He knew God's plan for him to be king; however, he waited. And he trusted (1 Samuel 24).

In Psalm 31:24, David pens these words:

"Be strong, and let your hearts take courage, all you who wait for the LORD!" (ESV).

I have been in a season of waiting. I have cried out to God to deliver me. And I have waited, knowing that His plan is for my good but crying out for answers all the same.

In a similar verse, David reminds himself of truth, to be strong, courageous and wait.

"Wait for the LORD; be strong and let your heart take courage; wait for the LORD!" (Psalm 27:14 ESV).

Are you in a season of waiting or just coming out of one? Or has God used your waiting to prepare you for what's to come?

Let the words of this psalm and others like it keep you and encourage you in your waiting.

The Power to Wait

What happened during David's season of waiting? While he waited, he wrote psalms that still impact us and speak to us today. While he waited, God used that time to teach, minister and prepare him to lead Israel one day. He didn't know it then, but God would eventually use the outpouring of his heart — and his words spoken in agony — to help and heal people throughout history.

David waited well. We can, too, because of the power of the Lord Jesus Christ. He knows I struggle with this. And you may, too. However, He knows and provides the power we need to wait. And in the meantime, we can trust God while we're waiting for Him to act.

David waited with a humble heart. He didn't demand his way with God. Even when the Lord punished him for his sin with Bathsheba and for Uriah's murder, David acted humbly (see 2 Samuel 12).

The condition of our heart matters.

Waiting Takes Humility

In God's kingdom, there is no room for pride. It takes humility to recognize God knows best and He has everything under control, then to stand firm in our faith. Humbly waiting for God is not for the faint of heart. It requires unwavering courage. It takes strength and determination to resist trying to control situations ourselves. It takes humility to know when we need help from Almighty God.

Taken captive by the king of Babylon, Manasseh was in distress. Granted, he had brought this on himself. He was the son of Hezekiah, a good king who did right in the eyes of the Lord. But Manasseh was far from the king his father had been.

He did much evil, practicing sorcery, divination and witchcraft. He sacrificed his two sons, plus many other people, by fire, leading the people of Jerusalem astray.

God brought the army of the king of Assyria against him, who put a hook in his nose, bound him with shackles and carted him off to Babylon.

Do you ever think God's not listening?

We can be in distress for different reasons. It doesn't have to be the result of sin, as it was in Manasseh's case. But no matter the cause, God listens to us. The Lord even listened to this evil man's plea and was moved by his appeal.

"In his distress he sought the favor of the LORD his God and humbled himself greatly before the God of his ancestors. And when he prayed to him, the LORD was moved by his entreaty and listened to his plea; so he brought him back to Jerusalem and to his kingdom. Then Manasseh knew that the LORD is God" (2 Chronicles 33:12–13 NIV).

Not only did God listen, but He also restored Manasseh to his kingdom.

What made the difference? A humble heart. Manasseh had committed terrible sins. But when he cried out to God, God knew his heart.

God will provide for us; we just need to wait and act humbly.

Other scriptural figures also acted humbly, and God provided restoration for them as well.

- God had declared disaster on King Ahab. The Bible describes him as someone who sold himself to do evil in the eyes of the Lord, urged on by his wife Jezebel. Once Ahab humbled himself, however, God decided he would not bring disaster on Ahab in his day (see 1 Kings 21:25–26).
- Hezekiah cried out to the Lord when he learned that God had determined he was going to die. Because of his prayer and tears, God extended his life by 15 years (see 2 Kings 20).
- Manasseh's grandson, King Josiah, was only 26 when Hilkiah, the high priest, found the book of the Law that had been handed down from Moses. Josiah's heart was responsive to the words he read in the book, and he humbled himself before God (see 2 Chronicles 34:27).

God Meets Our Needs

The Israelites saw God's provision during their 40-year journey in the wilderness. He tested them and He provided for them. They always had food and clothes. Their feet didn't even swell. Did you know that God's manna followed the Israelites into the Promised Land, then ended the day after they arrived? Six days a week for 40 years, God provided manna for them. It arrived like clockwork, then ended the day it wasn't needed any longer. Talk about God's provision.

God pays attention to even the smallest details. He wrote a new law for the four daughters of Zelophehad, who had no sons to inherit his land. If these four daughters didn't marry, they would be without land to inherit (see Numbers 36).

This new law made sure their needs were met.

Do you need God's provision today? Or do you need a warrior to pray on your behalf?

God is the Alpha and Omega, the beginning and the end. He is the breath of life. He is our timeless redeemer. He is forever faithful. He is the Prince of Peace, the Lamb of God, the Lion of Judah. He is Jesus Christ our Lord.

And He is completely capable of meeting our needs. We need only wait and humble ourselves.

Giving God the Driver's Seat

The book of Numbers describes the Israelites' entry into Canaan, their Promised Land, which was described as a land flowing with milk and honey. They struggled with trust and waiting, too, deciding many times to take matters into their own hands. Because of their lack of faith, an 11-day journey took them 40 long years.

The same God who led them leads us, too. Dare we let go of the wheel and allow Him to take control?

At times, I've decided to trust God and wait on His provision, only to reverse that thought hours later so I can do it my way. Waiting is not my strong suit.

I pray for strength for us today to release our doubts, our fears, and even our decisions to Almighty God.

As we navigate our days, months and years, let's invite Jesus to take the wheel. Let's surrender and trust Him to meet our needs.

God Is Near

Do you have a need?

Do you need to experience the power of the Holy Spirit?

One day we will see Jesus face to face. In the meantime, we can live in the power of the Holy Spirit today.

We can find Him:

- when we are waiting
- when we need healing
- when our world comes crashing down
- when we're charging through a fire
- when we're fighting a battle

Wherever we go, He is beside us. Every moment of the day, He is near.

He is at work in every detail, even the smallest details of our lives.

"But Jesus replied, 'My Father is always working, and so am I'" (**John 5:17 NLT**).

My busyness has often blinded me from recognizing Jesus in my day. The truth is, He can show up whenever and wherever. He defends me and stands up for me, presenting me to the Father.

CHAPTER FIFTEEN

One Glorious Day

Quote:

"When you have laboriously completed your daily task, go to sleep in peace. We rest because he reigns."

— Victor Hugo

Scripture:

"You are worthy, our Lord and God, to receive glory and honor and power, for you created all things, and by your will they were created and have their being" (Revelation 4:11 NIV).

Songs:

"Made for More" by Josh Baldwin
"God Really Loves Us" by Crowder
"Trust in God" by Elevation Worship
"This Is Our God" by Phil Wickham

After a week-long meeting in San Diego, I was anxious to leave the building and breathe in fresh air. Outside the hotel, a bike rental company caught my eye. I compared a few routes and decided to take the 13-mile path to La Jolla. Drawing near to the destination, the route wove me through a neighborhood displaying the Pacific Ocean as its backdrop.

I stopped to watch the sun sink into the dark water. Residents strolled out of their homes to do the same. The fading light took my breath away, captivating my soul.

Sundown

Sundown can mean a closing chapter in your life. The end of a particular season.

A child's senior year of high school points to the end of a season in life. But it also points to an exciting new chapter. A wedding or a new job can do the same.

For me, sundown — the end of the day or the end of a season — brings about a new beginning and hope for tomorrow.

A New Beginning

Jesus' ministry on Earth did just that. With His sacrifice, the old covenant God handed down through Moses became obsolete.

Living under the old covenant, priests entered the sanctuary's outer room to carry on their ministry. But only the high priest could enter the inner room once a year. And he could not enter without a blood sacrifice for himself and the people.

When Jesus died on the cross, He was that day's — and all eternity's — sacrifice. Nailed to the cross during the morning sacrifice and dying at 3 p.m., the time of the evening sacrifice,

Christ made the ultimate sacrifice. He entered the Most Holy place once and for all by his own blood, offering eternal redemption (see Hebrews 9).

Christ entered Heaven itself to appear for us in God's presence (see the book of Jude).

"But as it is he has appeared once for all at the end of the ages to put away sin by the sacrifice of himself" (Hebrews 9:26 ESV).

Christ ended His season on Earth by sacrificing Himself to do away with sin. He began His next season when He sat down at the right hand of God (see Hebrews 10:12).

Hope for the Future

Are you at the end of a season? Can you peer beyond sundown in your life and see the hope that Christ brings through His sacrifice?

- Hope for salvation. You can receive Christ's gift today.
- Hope for a brighter future. Hold on to the hope His promises bring.
- Hope for peace. Trust His plan and receive peace.
- Hope for another day of strength. Claim the power of the Holy Spirit in your life.

Hope believes in a better tomorrow.

Make the most of the season you're in, and when a sundown comes, seize the new beginning and rest in the hope you have in Christ.

Heaven Is a Real Place

Kimberly experienced the beauty of this hope as she watched her dad leave this world and enter a new life in Heaven. Her reflections from the day of that event instill a message of encouragement and hope.

Wednesday morning:

We haven't had much sleep over the past eight or nine days. Bless Mom, she's had almost none.

Dad slept for several hours in his hospital bed, but it was a tough morning. The hospice nurse came to assess his condition. Still conscious, he was able to voice needs, but his condition was obviously declining.

A week before this, Dad told Mom about what he was seeing. "Oh, it's so beautiful . . ." Mom asked if it was beauty like landscaping, flowers and plants. He said, "Yes, but the architecture . . . oh, the architecture . . . "

That morning, Dad asked if we "saw that flash of light?" (Mom and I were both in the room and neither of us did.) Later, he saw a dove.

He told us there were angels all around in the room. Mom asked, "Angels around you?" Dad answered, "Angels around all of us" (meaning the three of us). He'd been looking up toward the ceiling and gently turning his head to look upward at various places in the room with a sense of awe, wonder and reverence on his face.

Words cannot describe just witnessing it all. To clarify, he wasn't under the influence of any meds when he described everything.

Wednesday night:

Mom prayed, asking God for divine intervention. As soon as she said, "In Jesus' name, Amen," Dad entered heaven's gates at 11:29 p.m. There was no doubt when he was ushered into the presence of Jesus. Heaven is a real place.

Kimberly and her mom were aware of God's presence surrounding them. They felt His support and comfort and reassurance of His love. Through her dad's eyes, she caught a glimpse of the beauty and joy that comes from being in the presence of God.

Presented with Great Joy

I have good news! One glorious day, Jesus will still be by our side when He presents us to the Father without fault and with great joy.

I have been taught all my life that Jesus is our advocate, that He redeems us and that because of our relationship with Him, we will be blameless before the Father. A verse in Jude takes it a step further. He will present us with great joy. I'm trying to wrap my head around that.

I don't typically think about Jesus having joy over me. Yes, I think He is pleased when we follow His will and His work for as long as we're here on Earth. But Jude goes deeper.

"To him who is able to keep you from stumbling and to present you before his glorious presence without fault and with great joy — to the only God our Savior be glory, majesty, power and

**authority, through Jesus Christ our Lord, before all ages, now
and forevermore! Amen"(Jude 24-25 NIV).**

For those who know Jesus — those who claim Him as
their Savior — He will present us to His glorious presence, the
Almighty God. He will present us without fault and with great
joy.

Think of it like a ballroom dance. For the male partner, it is
a presentation. It's not about him. His sole purpose is to present
his female partner on the dance floor. Every turn. Every step.
Every dip and twirl is meant to show her to others.

That's what Jesus will do for us one day. With pride, He will
present us to the Father.

This means that not only can we live a life of joy through a
relationship with Jesus Christ, but He will also have joy because
of us.

I am unworthy of God's grace, yet I am presented with joy.
Wow.

Friend, that puts a smile on my face.

**"But blessed are those who trust in the LORD and have made
the LORD their hope and confidence" (Jeremiah 17:7 NLT).**

Jesus Carries Us

Is anything too hard for the Lord?

I find my joy in the Lord Jesus Christ. He is Lord in all and
Lord over all.

He walks beside me, upholds me and carries me through my
life's journey.

Who else will go to bat for me like Him? Who else would
willingly give His life? Who else would leave their throne

and live among men so I could know God? How could I not surrender my life to Him?

Let's also not underestimate the word of God working on our behalf. God's word advocates for us, spreading hope and salvation across the world. It is alive and brings renewal to our souls. I am grateful for the healing power of God's word.

Yes, people can be good to us, encourage us and offer help. But no one brings the kind of hope Jesus does. No one will ever care for us like Jesus. His goodness surpasses our understanding. He offers unmatched hope and compassion.

We can depend daily on God's faithful promises, knowing Christ Himself intercedes for us in the Father's presence.

Love and Adoration

I think there is a moment when the busyness, the stress of all the preparation, the last-minute mishaps — and sometimes disasters — fall away when standing face to face reciting marriage vows. At that point, it's just the bride and her groom, completely immersed in love and adoration for each other, making their commitments and beginning a new life together.

I especially love seeing the groom see his bride for the first time. His expression speaks his heart. She captivates him.

Face to Face

Here's something to think about. The Bible tells us that one day soon Jesus will come for his bride, the church. That bride and groom moment will be reversed on the day we see Jesus face to face. We will gaze on Him with complete love and adoration. He alone will be our reward.

King of the World

Friends, the King of the World has chosen us and wants a relationship with us. As followers of Christ, He is our redeemer. When we choose to follow Jesus, he redeems us from

- shame and guilt
- feelings of failure
- low self-esteem
- our mistakes
- our pride
- and a host of other things

Don't let mistakes or mishaps take your joy from the One who loves you with an everlasting love. Instead, you can find joy

- in the Lord
- in the life-changing word of the Lord
- in new beginnings
- when challenges or disasters come your way
- when you praise Him

Let's be completely immersed in love and adoration for Jesus, our King of the World.

"Your words were found, and I ate them, and your words became to me a joy and the delight of my heart, for I am called by your name, O LORD, God of hosts" (Jeremiah 15:16 ESV).

"For Christ suffered for sins once for all, the righteous for the unrighteous, that he might bring you to God" (1 Peter 3:18 CSB).

A believer's stability for this life as well as confidence for eternity rests solely on the written promises of God's word.

Today, we wait to one day be with Jesus face to face. But we don't have to wait to know His presence. God's presence surrounds us no matter where we are or what happens in our day, in our week or in our lives. We can find confidence and assurance in Almighty God who is near.

"You make known to me the path of life; in your presence there is fullness of joy; at your right hand are pleasures forevermore" (Psalm 16:11 ESV).

What do you want to be known for at the end of your life?

Do you want to be known as someone who trusted God through every circumstance in life — like the many we've covered in the pages of this book?

Through each one, both in scripture and in personal examples, we have seen that God can be trusted. He is ever present, seeing you through each circumstance, situation or event in your life.

Change the Way You Think

Do you need a glimpse of who God is? I know I do.

And with faith in Jesus Christ and the knowledge He is with us, we can fight our battles with confidence. We can weather unforeseen storms. We can push through life's setbacks.

God is always there. He's right there in your story.

I pray that is exactly what we will find as we worship and acknowledge who God is. The God who meets us where we are — even in our questions. The God who is patient with us — even in our doubts and fears. And the God who walks beside us and encourages us — even when we lack strength and confidence.

Change the way you think. Let God transform you into a new person, and learn to see Him in your story.

"Don't copy the behavior and customs of this world, but let God transform you into a new person by changing the way you think. Then you will learn to know God's will for you, which is good and pleasing and perfect" (Romans 12:2 NLT).

WHAT'S NEXT?

Christmas came just three months after my husband passed away. Determined to incorporate joy into the day, I bought body-bubble soccer balls for my three sons. Picture oversized bubble wrap around your body. We filled the inflatable body-sized balls with air and went outside. My sons quickly transformed into living pinballs, ricocheting across our front lawn on that wet Christmas morning.

The spectacle was nothing short of comical. After the older brothers sent my youngest tumbling, he lay on his side, arms and legs flailing in the air, and repeatedly cried out, "I can't get up!" Neighbors stopped by just to watch the show.

It brought a bit of joy and a glimmer of hope to an otherwise dark day.

Wouldn't it be amazing if life came equipped with bubble balls to buffer us against life's cruel blows and bitter disappointments? This invisible barrier could soften the impact of life's painful moments and allow us to bounce back.

Tragedy will strike and trouble will come. They will absolutely bring us to our knees at times. As flawed individuals, we must take our own sin into account as well. But we can find hope and guidance through the character of God displayed in scripture.

Throughout the Bible, God demonstrates His steadfast love to His people. Psalm 106 opens with praise and thanksgiving.

The psalmist then recounts the Israelites historical lesson of their repeated sin, their provoking the Lord to anger, and God's deliverance and restoration:

"They exchanged the glory of God for the image of an ox that eats grass. They forgot God, their Savior, who had done great things in Egypt, wondrous works in the land of Ham, and awesome deeds by the Red Sea" (Psalm 106:20–22 ESV).

The scriptures tell us when God remembered His covenant, He relented according to the abundance of His steadfast love. The psalmist recalls many of their sins and confesses to God they have a pattern of being unfaithful to Him.

But God doesn't give up on them, despite their cycle of rebellion and unbelief. The psalmist goes on to say how important it is to remember God's works, to remember His love and to keep abiding in and obeying the Lord.

And that is the challenge for us today.

The stories in this book share one common thread — Jesus. Whether we face obstacles, mistakes, tragedies or moments of obedience, Jesus remains close, wraps himself around us and walks with us through every bump, tumble or cry of frustration. He's as close as a protective bubble ball wrapped tightly around us.

He is always there. It is we who are prone to wander. To counter this, we need to read His word and remember what He has done. God's word lights our path. It speaks to our hearts personally. Whether it's rescue from a storm, protection from danger, healing from emotional or physical injury, don't overlook the hand of God at work. It is not a blip on the screen of our past. It reminds us He remains ever present.

If you don't know Jesus personally, this would be a great time to receive His gift of life, His mercy and His grace, and show people what your new life is like and astonish them with your boldness and faithfulness.

I hope these stories have challenged you to look for God in your story. I hope they remind you of who God is, what He does and how He works in the story of our lives.

"Seek the LORD and His strength; seek His presence continually" (1 Chronicles 16:11 NASB1995).

ACKNOWLEDGMENTS

To my Lord and Savior Jesus Christ. My Rock, my sustainer, my provider, my hope and my comfort. Without my faith, I would be lost and without joy.

To my wonderful friends and family:

- Connor, Garrett and Parker — being your mom is one of my greatest adventures. My love for you knows no limits. Thank you for letting me share our stories.
- Sonny and Mattie Mercer (Mom and Dad) — thank you for modeling Jesus for me, for your unconditional support especially during my darkest days and supplying me with inspiration for my stories.
- My loving husband Matthew — you are always in my heart. So are our beautiful daughter Ashlynn and our four babies we never knew. And Syd and Sara Cameron, as well as my sweet friend Angie — until we meet again in God's presence.
- My sweet sisters who've responded to my many emails and texts asking you to review copy for me — Aimee Kane, Bonny Van, Carol Hendrix, Christy M., Elizabeth Cobb, Holly Campbell, Lisa Mencer, Liz Craft, Sarah Heatherly, Valerie Barley.
- Those who willingly shared their stories so that others could be encouraged and drawn closer to the Lord —

Lisa Mencer, Rachel Shelby, Lynne Free, Pearl Wise, Jennifer Bass, Mattie Mercer, Laurie Kent, Carol Hendrix, Christy M., Leesa McMillin, Cary Heyer, Blake Davis, Jennifer Douglas, Kimberly Stuckey.
- My nephew James Mencer, who I can always depend on to lend a technical hand.
- Those who provided your feedback, wisdom and insight — Liz Craft, Celeste Drost, Carol Hendrix, Rich Mencer, Rachel Shelby, Tara Thomas.

To everyone who has lifted me to the Father as I've continued down this book-writing journey. Sandy Miller, thank you for praying me through. You have the sweetest heart.

To Karen Pina and Kurt Bubna, my author success coaches as well as Beacon Point editing services for your guidance and perspective.

To everyone who helped me launch, promote and bring this book to life. It takes a village to make a book a reality!

ABOUT THE AUTHOR

Patricia Cameron is an author, speaker, Bible study leader and writer for her *Faith-Driven Joy* blog. Through her testimony, personal stories and scriptures, she guides women to seek hope, experience love, receive encouragement, and embrace joyful faith. The unexpected loss of her husband when he was 45 tested her faith, but God showed her she could find joy again. She shares her journey of rediscovering that joy in her book *Grief Unwrapped: Discovering Joy in a Season of Sorrow*. An adventurer at heart, Patricia loves traveling and anything outdoors, seeking to live life to the fullest. She has the honor and joy of raising three sons and holds her daughter in Heaven close to heart. You can find out more at patriciacameronwrites.com.

Connect with Patricia at patricia@faithdrivenjoy.com. She would love to hear your story of God's presence and how He worked in your life through it.

Follow Patricia on Social Media.

Facebook: https://www.facebook.com/faithdrivenjoy
Instagram: https://www.instagram.com/faithdrivenjoy/
X: https://x.com/faithdrivenjoy
Linktree: https://linktr.ee/patriciacameron

"EVER PRESENT" PLAYLIST

"How He Loves" by David Crowder Band
"God Is In This Story" by Katy Nichole & Big Daddy Weave
"Breathe" by Jonny Diaz
"All Joy No Stress" by Rhett Walker
"You've Already Won" by Shane & Shane
"Battle Belongs" by Phil Wickham
"I Just Need U" by TobyMac
"Heaven Help Me" by Zach Williams
"Scars in Heaven" by Casting Crowns
"Miracle Power" by We the Kingdom
"Just Be Held" by Casting Crowns
"I Will Carry You" by Ellie Holcomb
"God, Turn It Around" by Jon Reddick
"One Pair of Hands" by Carroll Roberson
"Honestly, We Just Need Jesus" by Terrian
"Abide" by Aaron Williams
"Trust and Obey"
"Need You Now (How Many Times)" by Plumb
"Tear off the Roof" by Brandon Lake
"There Was Jesus" by Zach Williams and Dolly Parton
"My Father Has It" by Landon Wolfe
"Made for More" by Josh Baldwin
"God Really Loves Us" by Crowder
"Trust in God" by Elevation Worship
"This Is Our God" by Phil Wickham

CAN YOU HELP?

Thank you for reading *Ever Present*!

I would love to hear your feedback on the book; it would help me improve any future books.

Please take a couple of minutes to leave a helpful review on Amazon.

Thanks so much!

Patricia Cameron

"Patricia has given us an 'Open Book' of God's mercy and grace through her 'Open Journey' in this book. Her personal stories and others' stories of experiencing the presence of God, along with the application of the Word of God will grab the heart of readers. Find your quiet place, a cup of your favorite blend and be spiritually energized and equipped for an extraordinary life!"

—**Dr. Dennis Swanberg,** America's Minister of Encouragement, DennisSwanberg.com

"Real Life. Relevant. Serious and Silly. Patricia Cameron hit a homerun! She appeals to all who are going through the trials and triumphs of life. Her stories always lead us back to God when detours have taken us on different paths. Her heart is to take us from the crisis to the peace found in Christ. What a JOY to read such a relatable book!"

—**Tammy Whitehurst,** Motivational Christian Speaker

"It's not always easy to see God in our own stories. Sometimes, we need a friend to help us realize just how near He is in the good days and the hard times, alike. Patrica Cameron is that friend! A gifted storyteller, Patricia uses Biblical lessons and real-life examples to help us rediscover the joy of finding Jesus in our everyday moments."

—**Shellie Rushing Tomlinson,** Bible teacher and author of *Seizing the Good Life*

"Patricia's heartfelt storytelling invites readers to recognize God's presence in their everyday lives, transforming ordinary moments into extraordinary encounters with Jesus. This book will inspire you to see your own story with new eyes and rediscover His loving presence throughout every season."

—**Robyn Dykstra,** International Speaker